Previous page:
Class 24 diesel No D5092 brings a train of oil tanks out of the tunnel at Canfield Place, Finchley Road on 21 May 1966. The tanks carried fuel for the DMU depot at Marylebone. *I.S. Krause*

Below:
Standard Class 5MT No 73053 works the 9.50 (Sundays) Marylebone to Nottingham between Rugby and Lutterworth on a crisp morning — 14 January 1962. *M. Mitchell*

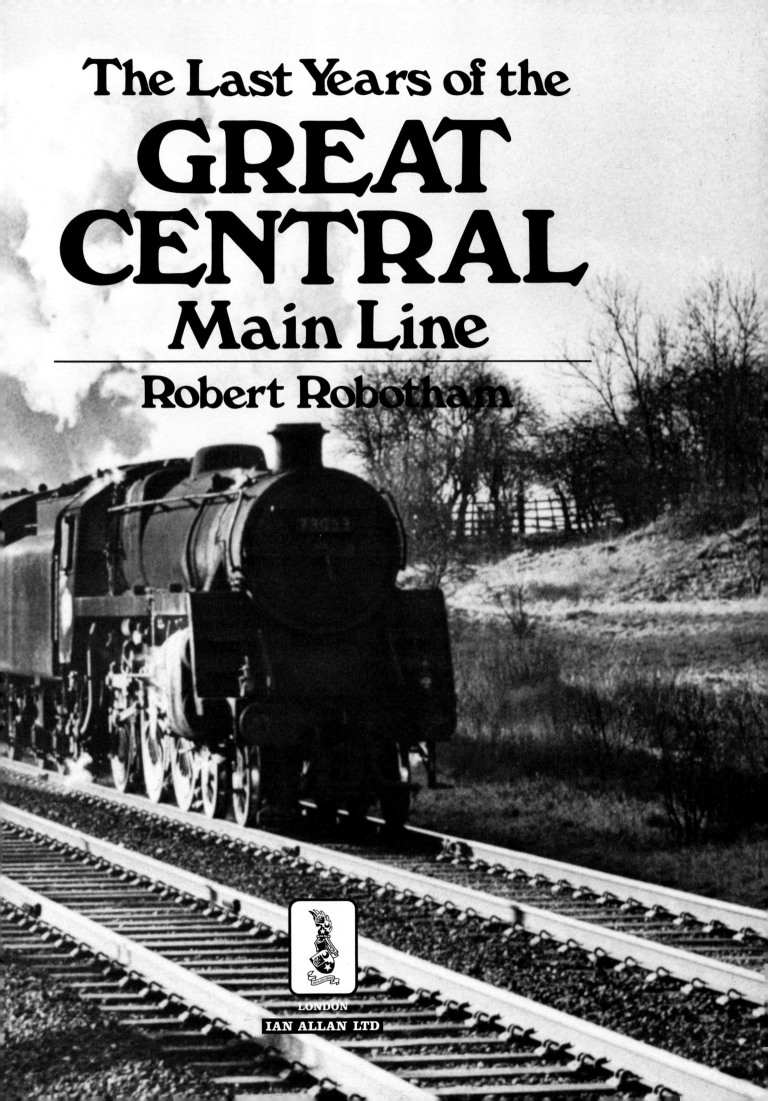

The Last Years of the
GREAT CENTRAL
Main Line

Robert Robotham

LONDON
IAN ALLAN LTD

First published 1986
Second impression 1988
Third impression 1997

ISBN 0 7110 1613 5

Published by Ian Allan Publishing

an imprint of Ian Allan Ltd, Terminal
House, Shepperton, Surrey TW17 8AS.
Printed by Ian Allan Printing Ltd, at its
works at Coombelands in Runneymede,
Surrey.

Code: 9711/A1

Front endpaper:
Class 9F 2-10-0 No 92092
approaches Princes Risborough
with an up Class 8 freight from
the GC line on 26 September
1964.   *B. Stephenson*

Rear endpaper:

'A3' Pacific No 60052 *Prince
Palatine* leaves Marylebone with
the down 'Master Cutler' in July
1952.   *Brian Morrison*

Contents

Preface

No other British railway was quite like the Great Central, both in the way it was constructed, and in the type of railwaymen it produced. Trains were driven in a way that was 'Great Central' in fashion – vigorously worked with fast, exciting accelerations and what can only be described as screeching stops as expresses approached stations. These habits were born of necessity; the Great Central was a fast and efficient rail link flanked on either side by other lines offering fierce competition for its traffic. Today the line is remembered with fondness – indeed it may be argued that some of the style of rail travel was lost with its closure. Few trains could match the service of the 'Master Cutler' – the flagship of Great Central passenger services. Freight traffic also was intense and, despite only having a double track to run on, the superb alignments and engineering of the line allowed very fast working.

This book is offered as a tribute to all those railwaymen – drivers, firemen, guards, locomotive inspectors, track gangers, signalmen, dining and buffet car staff, booking clerks and station staff – whose efforts, often in adverse conditions, made the Great Central the envy of other regions. I hope these pages will help to tell the tale of the last years of a truly remarkable railway, and offer inspiration to all of those who are restoring a section of the route that it is hoped will one day run in both Leicestershire and Nottinghamshire.

Acknowledgements
Special thanks are due to David Wellington, Rex Partridge and Cedric Spiller for providing the text for chapters 4, 5 and 7 respectively; and to Horace Gamble, Barry Hilton, David Holmes and Mike Mitchell for their assistance.

Robert Robotham
1986

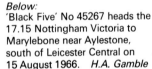

Below:
'Black Five' No 45267 heads the 17.15 Nottingham Victoria to Marylebone near Aylestone, south of Leicester Central on 15 August 1966. *H.A. Gamble*

Introduction

The Nationalisation of the 'Big Four' railway companies in 1948 produced the British Railways Regions, which were just as independent in their attitudes towards railway operating and marketing as they had been under private ownership. Indeed, the competition between routes such as Euston and Kings Cross to Scotland, Paddington and Waterloo to Exeter and Euston and Paddington to Birmingham still existed to a high degree amongst staff at all levels.

The Great Central London Extension to Marylebone and the Midland main line to St Pancras were no exception. Ever since passenger services began to Marylebone on 15 March 1899 the battle had been on. However, despite being the last main line into London, and therefore having to start competing against companies which were already firmly established in the market place, the Great Central managed, thanks to very high quality advertising and fast running, to win a respectable share of business. This success was attributable to the top management team of the Great Central which was formed by some most imaginative railwaymen, led by chairman Alexander Henderson. The work of men such as J.G. Robinson, the Chief Mechanical Engineer, Sam Fay, the General Manager, Joseph Rostern, the Line Superintendent and A.F. Bound, the head of the signalling department, ensured that the Great Central won a high reputation amongst its customers.

It is true to say that the other railway companies were not pleased with the building of the Great Central. It competed directly (and in virtual parallel geographically) with the Midland main line, and provided a shorter route between Nottingham and Leicester. Without the diversion via Derby that the Midland suffered, all Great Central expresses could call at Nottingham and Leicester, the two cities in the East Midlands that provided the vast majority of revenue and potential. Despite a slightly longer route to Sheffield, Great Central expresses were smartly timed, the fastest service being the 2hr 50min 'Sheffield Special' afternoon flyer from Marylebone. The Great Central also attracted business from the Great Northern Kings Cross to Sheffield via Retford route, and from the London & North Western from Manchester and Rugby, though in these latter cases, to a lesser extent.

The link from the Great Central at Woodford Halse to the Great Western at Banbury also gave the opportunity for cross country services, the most famous of these being the York to Bournemouth express which continued to run up until closure in 1966. Both the Banbury connection and the link into the Stratford & Midland Junction line to Stratford-upon-Avon saw vast amounts of freight traffic. Large quantities of materials, notably coal from the Nottinghamshire and South Yorkshire areas, passed through the system via the two marshalling yards at Annesley and Woodford Halse. The accommodation of inter-regional traffic, in addition to Great Central main line services, on a two-track system

(a) Chesterfield Central
(b) Eydon Road Platform
(c) Chacombe Road Platform
(d) Banbury
(e) Akeman Street
(f) Wotton
(g) Ashendon Junction
(h) Haddenham
(i) Ilmer Halt
(j) Princes Risborough
(k) Saunderton
(l) High Wycombe
(m) Beaconsfield
(n) Seer Green
(o) Gerrards Cross
(p) Denham Golf Club
(q) Denham
(r) Northolt Junction
(s) Northolt Park
(t) Sudbury Hill
(u) Sudbury
(v) Wembley Hill

Sheffield Victoria
Beighton
Killamarsh
Eckington
Staveley Town
(a) Duckmanton Junction
Heath Junction
Pilsley
Tibshelf Town
Kirkby Bentinck
Hucknall Central
Bulwell Common
New Basford
Nottingham Victoria
Nottingham Arkwright St
Ruddington
Rushcliffe Halt
East Leake
Loughborough Central
Quorn & Woodhouse
Rothley
Belgrave & Birstall
Leicester Central
Whetstone
Ashby Magna
Lutterworth
Rugby Central
Braunston & Willoughby
Charwelton
Woodford Halse
(b) Culworth
(c) Helmdon
(d) Brackley Central
Finmere
Calvert
Grendon Underwood Jct
(e) Quainton Road
(f) Aylesbury Town
(g) Stoke Mandeville
(h) Wendover
(i) Great Missenden
(j) Amersham
(k) Chalfont & Latimer
(l) Chorley Wood
(m) Rickmansworth
(n) Moor Park
(o) Northwood
(p) Northwood Hills
(q) Pinner
(r) North Harrow
(s) Harrow-on-the-Hill
(t) Northwick Park
(u) Preston Road
(v) Wembley Park
Neasden South Jct
Willesden Green
Marylebone

required tight timings and careful pathing and as a consequence both passenger and goods trains ran at high speeds. The exemplary operational standards ensured that express passenger and freight trains could pass busy locations such as Rugby and Leicester with minimal delays and speed restrictions. The line was also the only main route built to full Berne loading gauge and had no level crossings once past Beighton. Sir Edward Watkin, the chairman of the Great Central and the Metropolitan railways at the conception of the London Extension project, had originally intended the line to pass through London and continue to the Channel ports but, as in many cases of building new lines, lack of funds precluded the goal.

The aggressive competition and the undoubted hostility of other railway companies towards the Great Central created a fiercely independent spirit amongst its staff. This spirit continued into LNER days and right through to nationalisation when, still under Eastern Region control, the line competed for business with the London Midland.

For how long, however, could this competition and duplication of routes be allowed to continue in a national rail network, now itself under fierce attack from roads and airlines? It was found in the conclusions of the Beeching Report that the capacity of the railway network throughout the country was far greater than required and certainly the retention of two routes to the East Midlands could not be justified. Strong cases could be argued for the retention of either the Great Central or the Midland (and indeed for the closure of both), but the identity of the intended victim did not become obvious until the London Midland Region took control of the Great Central from 1 February 1958. Almost immediately the line was downgraded to a secondary route, and from 2 January 1960 the expresses were withdrawn and replaced by semi-fast trains between Marylebone and

Nottingham. Most of the smaller stations were closed, leaving a rather unattractive service.

Thus the last main line became the first major victim of the many closure proposals after Beeching. At the time it was seen as a necessary sacrifice helping, it was presumed, to secure the future of Britain's railways by putting them on a more profitable footing. It is only in the last 20 years that the folly of the closure of the GC can be seen. The opening of the Channel Tunnel would have seen the line develop as a mover of continental loading gauge freight and passenger services to Manchester with important links through the Midlands. Towns such as Brackley, Lutterworth and Ashby Magna have grown greatly in size and suburban stations around Sheffield, Nottingham and Leicester would have been well used as the car is increasingly clogging up these cities every day. But in the 1960s that was not foreseen and such was the hostility from the LMR to the GC that any hope of a reprieve or even 'mothballing' was out of the question.

Closure of the GC as a through route was a great waste of a national asset and if ever, in the future, government and railwaymen need to adjust the rail network a long term view of demography and freight prospects should be undertaken, without any 'inter-regional' scores being settled. The GC was a classic victim of this policy — if only it had clung on until the mid-1970s, in the author's view, it would still be operating today.

Below:
Inside the cavern of Nottingham Victoria looking south up platform 7 on 15 January 1964. Passengers await the 12.48 to Bournemouth West.
H.A. Gamble

the line from the Western Region at Banbury joined the main line at Culworth Junction. The Banbury branch was used by through expresses, freights and the Woodford–Banbury link service known as the 'Banbury Motor' – usually a tank locomotive and one or two coaches – certainly providing a great contrast to the expresses. There were two stations between Banbury and Culworth Junction – Eydon Road Platform and Chacombe Road Platform (closed 2 April 1956 and 6 February 1956 respectively) that served small hamlets along the route. Culworth Junction was on a high embankment in the middle of nowhere and was a lonely spot for the signalman.

After Culworth Junction the line reached one of the most important areas on the Great Central route – Woodford Halse. The Stratford & Midland Junction line crossed over the Great Central south of the station and gained access via a short spur. Woodford's yards were on either side of the main line, and were usually packed with wagons and locomotives either shunting or awaiting departure with trains. The locomotive depot was situated on the eastern side of the Great Central and was notable for its high coaling stage. As recently as 1941, the 'New Yards' were added again either side of the main line, and were largely used for wartime traffic, but continued in importance after hostilities finished. Despite its size as a railway junction, Woodford was passed at normal line speed after which the line ran on to

Charwelton. Charwelton was famous for its water troughs, and, also on a local basis, its 'Charwelton Week', which in summer 1958 provided many problems to Great Central services as much of the livestock that took part also decided to take walks along the line, mostly to drink at the water troughs! Most expresses picked up water at Charwelton and then curved right through the station towards the cutting leading to Catesby tunnel. The tunnel was 3,000yd long and dropped on a gradient of 1 in 176 towards the north end. It was also very wet in parts. Catesby's north portal was near to Catesby House, famous for its association as a meeting place for Guy Fawkes and his fellow rogues before their antics in London. From the tunnel the line descended at 1 in 176 for the next 7½ miles, and on its way crossed Catesby viaduct – 12 arches over the river Leam – Staverton viaduct and passed Staverton Road box. At the bottom of the descent from the Northamptonshire uplands lay Braunston & Willoughby station, north of which trains ran parallel with the Oxford canal on embankments towards Rugby Central which was approached through the deep Dunsmore cutting.

Rugby Central to Leicester Central

Rugby Central was in fact situated nowhere near to the centre of Rugby itself and was out of sight in a typical Great Central cutting. It had two long sidings each 500ft in

Above left:
SR West Country Pacific No 34002 *Salisbury* heads an RCTS. 'Great Central Railtour' through Culworth Junction on 13 August 1966. The Banbury line ran off to the right here. *J. Scrace*

Left:
The 16.25 Marylebone to Nottingham passes Culworth on 14 April 1962 with 'K3' No 61910 in charge. *M. Mitchell*

Above:
Just north of Charwelton was Catesby Tunnel from which two '9Fs' (Nos 92011 and 92032) emerge with a Class H freight train on 20 May 1964. The destination is Woodford. *P.F. Fleming*

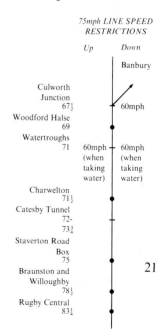

75mph LINE SPEED RESTRICTIONS

	Up	*Down*
		Banbury
Culworth Junction 67½		60mph
Woodford Halse 69		
Watertroughs 71	60mph (when taking water)	60mph (when taking water)
Charwelton 71½		
Catesby Tunnel 72-73¾		
Staverton Road Box 75		
Braunston and Willoughby 78½		
Rugby Central 83¾		

length to hold the many freights that intermingled with the passenger services. Despite having a fairly large population to serve, the Great Central station was the standard island platform type, and unlike the rival London & North Western station, had no speed restrictions. Running out of Rugby Central, the line continued through the cutting and out down a 1 in 176 gradient towards the celebrated 'Birdcage Bridge' over the LNWR, and thence on to the viaduct over the Oxford canal. Then began a climb passed Shawell box to the summit at the 88½ mile post and into the Lutterworth 'dip'. After Lutterworth station, the line climbed to mile post 91¾, and the descent began through Ashby Magna, down Ashby bank. Just north of Ashby Magna, the line crossed the Leicester Midland to Rugby Midland line, but the biggest unnatural feature noticeable on the Great Central between Lutterworth and Leicester was the new M1 motorway; indeed the Great Central track bed is still visible from it today. Ashby bank was between eight and nine miles long at a gradient of 1 in 176 and, as a result, passenger trains reached high speeds on the descent. Even up trains performed impressively due to the easy nature of the track alignment. Near the bot-

tom of the descent at 1 in 176, Whetstone station, on the southern outskirts of Leicester, was passed and then the line crossed the overbridge of the Midland's Leicester to Birmingham line. The Great Central then crossed the river and Grand Union Canal from which it passed through the suburbs of Glen Parva and Aylestone, crossing the canal again, and also the river Soar. Then, after crossing under the Coalville route from Knighton, the line passed Leicester South Goods box and, with it, Leicester yards and locomotive shed. After the yards, the Great Central ran on to the famous blue brick viaducts towards Leicester Central station. These marvellous structures were built of the finest materials in traditional Great Central fashion and consisted of 97 arches and 11 plate girders along with three lattice deck girder bridges over the canal and rivers. Leicester Central was formed of one large island platform with a double track bay at either end. The station buildings were not set above the rails, but set over to the east side, the platforms being reached by means of a subway. The buildings in Great Central Road, Leicester still stand today, and are fairly well preserved. On the station layout side, there were passing loops outside the platform roads to

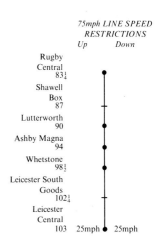

75mph LINE SPEED RESTRICTIONS

	Up	Down
Rugby Central 83¼		
Shawell Box 87		
Lutterworth 90		
Ashby Magna 94		
Whetstone 98½		
Leicester South Goods 102¼		
Leicester Central 103	25mph	25mph

24

allow the many freights through and, of course, the inevitable locomotive sidings that housed the large numbers of machines that awaited to relive other engines. Leaving for the north, the most striking feature was the large painted roof of the Great Central Hotel, the scene of many 'last drinks' before dashing for the train home.

Leicester Central to Nottingham Victoria

Leicester to Loughborough is one of the most scenic parts of the Great Central, and overall to Nottingham was one of the fastest sections of the route. The climb out of Leicester Central was initially over the blue brick viaduct and then through Abbey Lane sidings to Birstall which was reached after running on a high embankment through the northern outskirts of the city. The station at Belgrave & Birstall is situated on a curve and up trains passed through at high speeds on the descent to Leicester.

Once over the top of the climb at mile post $106\frac{1}{2}$, the line passed into the Charnwood Forest area, and on to Rothley, the village firmly planted in the Leicestershire stockbroker belt. Just north of Leicester, came Swithland sidings and the branch off to Mountsorrel for the quarries. At Swithland, the Great Central up and down main lines parted slightly and swept around an

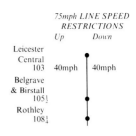

75mph LINE SPEED
RESTRICTIONS
Up   Down

Leicester
Central
103   40mph   40mph
Belgrave
& Birstall
$105\frac{1}{2}$
Rothley
$108\frac{1}{4}$

Above left:
'Black Five' No 44835 crosses the River Soar on the way out of Leicester with the 16.38 Marylebone to Nottingham on 12 July 1966.   *M. Mitchell*

Bottom left:
'V2' No 60961 of York shunts vans for the 11.15 Nottingham to Marylebone parcels at Leicester Central on 20 June 1964.
H. A. Gamble

Left:
'B1' No 61187 hurries past Belgrave & Birstall with the 8.40am Nottingham–Marylebone on 24 July 1961.   *M. Mitchell*

imaginary platform and over a bridge just close to the reservoir. Originally intended to be a station for the Swithland area, plans did not materialise and the platform was never built. The line strode across the Swithland reservoir on a viaduct and thence through a cutting and out of the woods and on to the Quorn straight, still on a falling gradient of 1 in 264. Once through the island platform at Quorn & Woodhouse station, the line descended towards Loughborough on a grade of 1 in 176 and passed through the station on a gentle right hand curve towards the bridge over its great rival, the Midland. Having passed the Brush Works, the route climbed to Barnston tunnel via a very high embankment which included a short viaduct over the river Soar. Once through Barnston's north portal, the line dropped towards East Leake station,

Above:
'K3' No 61872 races through East Leake on 29 June 1962 with the 15.30 Hull to Plymouth fish train. *D. Holmes*

Left:
Ivatt 4MT 2-6-0 No 43155 is on the Gotham branch with the 09.42 from Queen's Walk on 10 December 1962. The guard has just shut the crossing gates and No 43155 prepared to leave for the GC main line. *D. Holmes*

which was beautifully set in trees at the end of a deep cutting.

Rushcliffe Halt and the sidings for the British Gypsum establishment at Hotchley Hill were followed by Gotham Junction and the short branch to the Gotham British Gypsum factory. A quarter of a mile north of Gotham box, the line flattened out and ran on virtually flat grades passed the Ministry of Defence Depot at Ruddington and through the station down towards Nottingham. After passing near Wilford, the line ran on a high embankment towards the river Trent passing the Notts Forest cricket ground on the east side, mentioned due to there being a signal opposite the pitch, and the scene of many a minute's cricket watched by train crews while awaiting a clear road. Signals on this section were of an 'approach lit' type. In effect, when no trains were near the signal, it showed no light at all but, when a train was on section, the signal showed the correct aspect. After the train had passed, all lights went out once more.

The line then ran on to the four-track girder bridge and passed Trent Lane Junction and Nottingham goods yard before running on to another Great Central blue brick viaduct towards Arkwright Street (later to become the terminus of the truncated DMU Nottingham–Rugby service from September 1967). The viaduct then continued to a large 170ft girder bridge that spanned Nottingham Midland station, and over the canal to Weekday Cross Junction (situated on the viaduct) where the Great Northern line from Grantham joined for the run through the double track tunnel and into the huge cavern that housed Nottingham Victoria – one of the true railway 'cathedral' stations. Nottingham Victoria – known as 'the Vic' – was situated in the centre of Nottingham, unlike the Midland station, and had two large island platforms each nearly a quarter of a mile long and with bays at both ends. Like Leicester Central, there were loops for the freights and even a turntable with locomotive sidings. The platform buildings were as grand

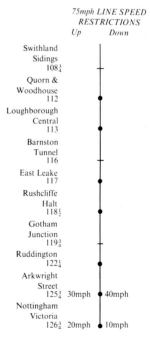

75mph LINE SPEED
RESTRICTIONS
Up   Down

Swithland
Sidings
108¾

Quorn &
Woodhouse
112

Loughborough
Central
113

Barnston
Tunnel
116

East Leake
117

Rushcliffe
Halt
118½

Gotham
Junction
119¾

Ruddington
122¼

Arkwright
Street
125¾   30mph   40mph

Nottingham
Victoria
126¾   20mph   10mph

as the main facade of the station with a large clocktower (that still stands today) that fronted on to Mansfield Road. The Great Central gave Nottingham its through NE/SW trains, still missing today with an absurd change at Derby now required. The 'Runners' and 'Windcutters' were just as impressive as the top passenger services and quite frequently stormed through the centre platform roads filling the station with a tremendous noise that echoed from the roof. Leicester to Nottingham was one of the fastest sections of the Great Central main line, most expresses running to near mile-a-minute timings, the fastest recorded being that of 86mph by '9F' 2-10-0 No 92164 and driver Ken Davies near Ruddington on the 18.18 Marylebone–Sheffield 'Master Cutler' in the summer of 1958. It was the last summer the 'Cutler' ran on the Great Central.

Nottingham Victoria to Sheffield Victoria

Leaving Nottingham Victoria, the Great Central entered Mansfield Road Tunnel and then passed Carrington station and ran straight into Sherwood Rise tunnel. In fact, Carrington was situated straight between the tunnel portals. The line climbed from Sherwood Rise, and turned towards Bulwell

Common, reached after crossing the river Leem on a typical Great Central blue brick viaduct. Then came the climb of 1 in 130 to 1 in 132 up to Hucknall Central and on to Annesley Junction and tunnel. Here was Annesley shed, famous for providing locomotives for the Woodford freights, and the yards where the coal and merchandise were marshalled for the run south. Annesley depot's crews did not just live in the local areas but also came from surrounding districts and, to cater for them, a special train was run between Bulwell Common and the depot. The famous Annesley 'Dido' was usually formed of any spare locomotive and some of the oldest stock around, but it was considered suitable for train crews! From Annesley the line dropped to Kirkby Bentinck and down to New Hucknall sidings and then climbed up to Tibshelf Town and Pilsley. After Pilsley came Heath and the loop off the Chesterfield Central that rejoined the main line at Staveley Town South Junction. The Great Central ran on a falling gradient, the steepest being 1 in 100, as it descended through Springwood Tunnel to Duckmanton. The route to Chesterfield followed the Rother valley and, once in the town, climbed steeply out through a tunnel towards the main line. The station had two

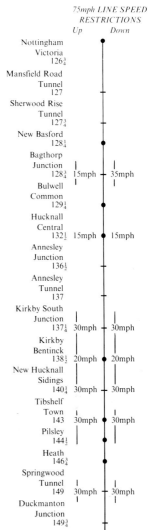

75mph LINE SPEED
RESTRICTIONS
Up   Down

	Up	Down
Nottingham Victoria 126¾		
Mansfield Road Tunnel 127		
Sherwood Rise Tunnel 127¾		
New Basford 128¼		
Bagthorp Junction 128¾	15mph	35mph
Bulwell Common 129¼		
Hucknall Central 132¼	15mph	15mph
Annesley Junction 136¼		
Annesley Tunnel 137		
Kirkby South Junction 137¼	30mph	30mph
Kirkby Bentinck 138½	20mph	20mph
New Hucknall Sidings 140¼	30mph	30mph
Tibshelf Town 143	30mph	30mph
Pilsley 144½		
Heath 146¾		
Springwood Tunnel 149	30mph	30mph
Duckmanton Junction 149¾		

Above left:
'B1s' Nos 61316 and 61183 run over the girder bridge that crosses the Trent near Nottingham with the 14.10 Manchester to Marylebone on 26 August 1954. *J.P. Wilson*

Far left:
'9F' No 92042 passes through the cathedral-like roof of Nottingham Victoria with a down iron ore train on 29 August 1964. *J.S. Hancock*

Left:
'8F' 2-8-0 No 48304 leaves Sherwood Rise Tunnel near New Basford station at 18.56 on Monday 29 July 1963 with a down train of empty coal wagons from Woodford to Annesley. *T. Boustead*

29

were closed, and, as with the expresses, were replaced by the Nottingham–Marylebone semi-fasts.

Cross-Country Services

The Great Central link to the Great Western between Woodford Halse and Banbury allowed long distance through services to pass from the South-West, South Wales and the South to the Midlands and the North with ease. Many of these trains had run since Great Central days (the line from Woodford to Banbury having opened in 1900), the most famous being the York to Bournemouth (and vice versa) express, which lasted right through to the end of the Great Central railway as a through route. The York to Bournemouth on its northern run was rostered for a Western Region locomotive as far as Leicester, which worked back on a local service later in the day. Summer Saturdays of course saw an even larger amount of through services, from South Yorkshire and Nottinghamshire to the south coast and West Country. It was, therefore, common for Leicester Central and even Nottingham Victoria to be graced by the presence of a Western engine, and occasionally even a Southern locomotive reached the two cities. In the reverse direction, Leicester Central locomotives worked through to Oxford and even Swindon.

By September 1966 all these services had been transferred via Birmingham New Street and the Midland line from Bristol to Derby and Sheffield but, as previously mentioned, the York to Bournemouth lasted to the final day.

Special Traffic and Diversionary Workings

With the railways now under national ownership, Marylebone became available as a reserve terminus and was first used as such in 1951 taking some of Euston's parcels trains, which then travelled via Calvert and the wartime spur to Bletchley and thence to the West Coast main line. The relief of Euston became even more important during the electrification of the West Coast route in the early 1960s, Marylebone also taking the Manchester sleeper and various other parcels services.

The Great Central route was also fortunate to pass close by the Wembley stadium on its way out of London. This of course brought numerous specials to the line whenever there were cup finals or other large attractions at the stadium. The Rugby League cup finals brought specials from the North to London and with them came the inevitable 'foreign' locomotives, usually 'V2s' but also a number of 'Jubilee' 4-6-0s. The most interesting event from the railway point of view was the Women's Hockey International which brought locomotives from the Western and Southern regions. As far as soccer matches were concerned, Leicester City played at Wembley in both 1961 and 1963, and Nottingham Forest in 1959; both appearances inevitably brought more specials, hauled mostly by 'Jubilees'

Below:
'Black Five' No 44872 enters Brackley Central, Northamptonshire on the Nottingham to Neasden parcels vans. The vans had travelled down the night before laden with newspapers and returned the following day. The date is 2 September 1966, one day before closure. *J.M. French*

Left:
'B1' 4-6-0 No 61271 approaches
Woodford Halse with the 13.40
from Marylebone on 23 May
1959. The S&MJ line crosses the
GC main line just behind the
train. *M. Mitchell*

and 'Royal Scots'. Perhaps the strangest locomotive to visit the Great Central was the 'GT3', a gas-turbine powered machine which, in 1961, was extensively tested over a six-month period. It cannot have been too popular with the line maintenance staff however, as it produced very hot exhaust fumes which set fire to Northgate Street bridge in Leicester and damaged signal and telecommunications equipment in other areas.

One of the most intriguing developments of the Great Central services came in early 1953 with the launch of a bargain overnight service to Scotland known as the 'Starlight Special', at a fare of just £3 10s (£3.50) return. The services aimed to compete with overnight road coaches and ran with an all-night buffet car. Loadings were fairly high and they often ran with reliefs in the sum-mer and at bank holidays. However, the 'Starlight Specials' were terminated in 1962 as a result of the review of coaching stock usage and also because it was suspected that they drew patronage off BR's own sleeper services. Marylebone also handled Motorail traffic to Glasgow and a relief service to Perth and continued to handle a Stirling service until the transfer of all Motorail ser-vices to Kensington Olympia.

Inevitably, the railway enthusiast needed little time to realise the ultimate fate of the Great Central, and this drew numerous specials which ran before closure. Notable appearances were 'Princess Coronation' Class 8P 4-6-2 No 46251 *City of Notting-ham,* the Midland Compound No 1000, No 4472 *Flying Scotsman* (a one time stable-mate at Leicester Central), Drummond 'T9' No 30120 in LSWR livery accompanied by

Far left:
'B1' 4-6-0 No 61041 runs out of
Dunton Bassett Tunnel on
29 August 1959 with the
Newcastle to Bournemouth West.
The train is going very slowly and
the driver and fireman are
struggling to improve the fire.
B.O. Hilton

Below:
'Black Five' 4-6-0 No 44872
passes Northwood on the
Metropolitan and Great Central
joint line with the 16.38
Marylebone to Nottingham on
the penultimate day of operation,
2 September 1966.
E.J.S. Gadsden

Class N 2-6-0 No 31790, and SR 'Schools' Class No 30925 *Cheltenham,* which incidentally, worked back south next day on the 12.30 semi-fast from Nottingham Victoria to Marylebone.

The 'Semi-Fasts'

From January 1960 there were only three daytime semi-fast services in each direction on the Great Central main line. These consisted of only six coaches with no refreshment facilities and the service pattern continued virtually unchanged until the closure. No Great Central trains ran via High Wycombe except for diversions due to engineering work. Initially, these semi-fasts fitted into the pattern of the remaining local trains that still ran between Aylesbury and Nottingham. When the smaller stations such as Quorn, Rothley and Belgrave & Birstall were closed in March 1963, the semi-fasts were retimed to make them, in

effect, substitute locals timed for commuters mainly on the Nottingham, Loughborough and Leicester axis. All, apart from the 17.15 ex-Nottingham, ran as four coaches only, the 17.15 having seven. The 08.38 from Marylebone also ran as a DMU for a while.

The LMR's influence had also brought a change of motive power. Leicester Central's shed declined significantly in importance, being retained to provide power for the cross country services and, up to 1963, the locals. Annesley and Neasden provided the power for the semi-fasts which consisted of many different types of locomotives, notably the ex-LMS 'Royal Scot' 4-6-0s that were unfortunately worn out. A few 'Britannia' Pacifics were also allocated to the Great Central line to cope not only with the traditional overnight mail trains (including Manchester to Marylebone), but also the diverted Manchester sleeping car train and additional summer traffic. As with the

'Royal Scots', their condition was not good and they were seen very much as the 'cast-offs' from the rest of the BR system. Annesley depot had done its best to revive the 'Britannias', transferred to it on Neasden's closure in 1962, but their improved condition saw them quickly transferred to other duties, leaving the worn out older LMS 'Black Fives', BR '9Fs' and the remaining 'Royal Scots' to cope. The condition of the motive power did not help the reliability of the services, and long delays could occur due to failures, when no back up power was immediately available. By 1965 the LMS 'Black Five' was the mainstay of the services with the few inevitable exceptions.

Summer 1965 saw Annesley as the only shed on the Great Central railway to remain open, ridiculous if a locomotive failed at the London end of the line. Cricklewood depot on the Midland route had taken over servicing on Neasden's closure in 1962 and responsibility was transferred to Willesden in December 1965 (though Willesden had been responsible for rectifying failures since Neasden's demise). Even making Banbury (now under London Midland Region control) reponsible for the maintenance and supply of motive power, did little to help solve the problem. Due to station and signalbox closures, a failure that occurred between stations or boxes inevitably meant long delays whilst the train crew tried to get assistance. A brief return of the 'Britannias' in the autumn of 1965 did little to help and the 'Black Fives', now allocated to Colwick in Nottinghamshire after the closure of Annesley, soldiered on, continuing to provide the mainstay of the power until the last semi-fast ran on 3 September 1966 and was replaced by the DMU service that ran between Nottingham and Rugby only. This lasted until 5 May 1969 and ran only to the hastily re-opened Arkwright Street station in Nottingham, pressed into service when Nottingham Victoria closed two years earlier on 2 September 1967.

Below left:
An excursion handbill for a 1962 day trip from Rugby to Sutton-on-Sea and Mablethorpe.

Below:
At Nottingham Victoria on 13 August 1960 'L1' 2-6-4T No 67775 is arriving with the 13.37 from Grantham under a magnificent gantry of lower-quadrant signals. *D.P. Leckonby*

Bottom:
'Jubilee' No 45622 *Nyasaland* is in immaculate external condition on Ashby Bank on 25 May 1963, as she is seen heading for Marylebone with a FA Cup Final special from Leicester.

PLEASE RETAIN THIS BILL FOR REFERENCE   L92/R(S/Adex)

WHITSUNTIDE HOLIDAYS : : 1962

DAY TRIP

T O

SUTTON-on-SEA

A N D

MABLETHORPE

TUESDAY 12th JUNE 1962

FROM	TIMES OF DEPARTURE	RETURN FARES Second Class	ARRIVAL TIMES ON RETURN
	am	s d	pm
RUGBY Central	8 36	21/6	10 52
LUTTERWORTH	8 48	18/3	10 40
WHETSTONE	9 0	17/-	10 24
LEICESTER Central	9 12	16/-	10 12
BELGRAVE & BIRSTALL ...	9 18	16/-	10 5
LOUGHBOROUGH Central ...	9 30	16/-	9 53
EAST LEAKE	9 38	14/6	9 43
RUSHCLIFFE HALT ...	9 42	14/6	9 37
RUDDINGTON ...	9 50	14/6	9 29
	pm	Passengers return same day at ...	pm
SUTTON-ON-SEA ... arrive	12 15		7 1
MABLETHORPE ... ,,	12 22	,, ,, ,,	6 54

CHILDREN under three years of age, free; three and under fourteen, half-fare. Fractions of a 1d. to be charged as a 1d.

TICKETS CAN BE OBTAINED IN ADVANCE AT STATIONS AND OFFICIAL RAILWAY AGENTS

Further information will be supplied on application to Stations, Official Railway Agents, or to Mr. L. A. METCALF, District Commercial Manager, Leicester. Telephone 23841, Extn. 34; or to Mr. H. BULLOUGH, District Commercial Manager, Derby. Telephone: Derby 42442, Extn. 204; or Mr. A. S. MEAD, District Passenger Manager, 43 Smallbrook, Ringway, Birmingham. Telephone: MIDland 2711.

May, 1962
BR35000

LONDON MIDLAND

(PX2/Adex)

Arthur Gaunt & Sons (Printers) Ltd., Heanor, Derbyshire.

Top:
'Black Five' No 45301 has arrived at Nottingham Victoria with the 09.20 Leicester Central to Mablethorpe on 22 August 1964. Another locomotive has backed on to the rear of the train for the run to Mablethorpe. *H. A. Gamble*

Above:
'Black Five' No 45222 coasts down towards East Leake with the 17.20 Rugby to Nottingham local service on 31 May 1966. *M. Mitchell*

Right:
'Britannia' 4-6-2 No 70031 *Byron* pulls out of Nottingham Victoria with the 17.15 train to Marylebone on 7 September 1963. *J.S. Hancock*

46

Above:
'B1' 4-6-0 No 61033 *Dibatag* starts out of Rugby Central on Sunday 7 September 1958 with an excursion to Sutton-on-Sea and Mablethorpe.   *M. Mensing*

Left:
On 3 June 1964 'Royal Scot' No 46122 *Royal Ulster Rifleman* heads the 18.15 Nottingham–Rugby out of Leicester Central and passes '9F' No 92073 waiting on the loop with an Annesley–Woodford freight.
M. Mitchell

Below:
The driver of 'V2' No 60831 awaits the 'right away' at Leicester Central on 16 August 1958 with the 2.20pm Manchester–Marylebone.
Barry O. Hilton

Above:
'B1' 4-6-0 No 61063 on a light but most important duty on 22 March 1952. The train is seen at Bulwell Common where it called to pick up railwaymen for Annesley Depot. It was known as the 'Annesley Dido', this name coming from the fact that it ran day in, day out, and thus was abbreviated D.I.D.O. by railwaymen. *J.F. Henton*

Right:
Collett '14XX' 0-4-2T No 1455 takes water at Aylesbury after arriving as the 11.00 service from Princes Risborough on 10 June 1962. *L. Sandler*

Below:
No 1455 leaves Princes Risborough on the 14.25 Aylesbury–High Wycombe service on 10 June 1962. Note the Hawksworth flush-sided autocoach named *Thrush*. *L. Sandler*

Above:
'B1' No 61315 leaves Nottingham Victoria with a stopping service to Chesterfield on 28 October 1952. *J.F. Henton*

Left:
Class 47 diesel No D1779 approaches Calvert with a Cup Final special from Manchester Piccadilly to Wembley Hill on 1 May 1965. *Brian Stephenson*

Below left and bottom:
A contrast in motive power at Rugby Central on Sunday 7 September 1958: 'B1' 4-6-0 No 61380 shunted empty stock for an excursion to Hull and Goole; whilst recently introduced Class 40 diesel No D201 later passed with the outward 'Farnborough Flyer'.
Both M. Mensing

3

Freight Services

If Leicester Central was the heart of the Great Central passenger service, then Woodford Halse was certainly the heart of the freight service. The Great Central had always been used heavily for freight traffic — as with the passenger service, the link to Banbury allowing many through workings. There was also the link to the Stratford & Midland Junction line which crossed the main line at Woodford. Most of the services were run as express freights, with a small number of locals serving the intermediate stations. The most intense usage of the line was between Annesley yard in Nottinghamshire and Woodford Halse, where there were many trains which carried vast amounts of coal from the East Midlands to South Wales and an abundance of general goods trains and steel traffic from the North East to South Wales and the West. There were also the famous Great Central fish trains from Grimsby and Hull to South Wales again run as express freights.

The last years of the Great Central also saw the introduction of a most astounding innovation in the freight workings of British Railways. The Annesley to Woodford freight service, which ran mostly loose coupled, had been launched in 1947 and was the epitome of efficient working. About 44 northbound arrivals and 43 departures plus the 47 southern arrivals with 58 departures were handled to a very high standard

of discipline to ensure that crews and locomotives could cover a complete round trip within one shift. Indeed they had to operate to a higher standard than express passenger workings, for if the locomotives were late for their trains, they were simply cancelled. The freights ran on an 'out and back' principle, the time taken to wait for the return working from Woodford being kept to a minimum. These trains were known to the operators as 'Modified Class F' freights, and indeed proved highly efficient, an astonishing three quarters of a million wagons a year being passed through Woodford in the early 1950s.

The Great Central line offered the opportunity for high speed running, and these freights attained 50mph plus on most occasions. They became renowned throughout British Railways for their efficiency and speed and were nicknamed 'Windcutters' or 'Runners' by the railwaymen. With the arrival of the '9F' 2-10-0, a vastly efficient and reliable locomotive, the service improved still further, some locomotives managing two trips per day.

The vast quantities of loaded and empty coal wagons passing through to and from the Western Region at Woodford via the 'Windcutters' meant an increase in importance for the S&MJ line that crossed the Great Central at that location. Most traffic to use this route to the Western (which travelled via Fenny Compton to Stratford-

Below:
Class O1 No 63880 2-8-0, a GC veteran, approaches Rugby Central on 7 November 1956 with a down freight consisting of empty flat wagons. *M. Mensing*

upon-Avon thence to the WR line to Cheltenham and South Wales), was semifinished steel from Consett and Scunthorpe passing to Newport, and it was hauled almost exclusively by the War Department 2-8-0 locomotives, 28 of which were allocated to Woodford shed. A daily Dringhouses–Marylebone express freight and twice weekly Class C Guinness train from Newcastle to the Park Royal Brewery were the only two long distance freights to the London area, each using the High Wycombe line.

Other general merchandise traffic was also distributed from Woodford along the Great Central and, whilst Woodford saw between 40 and 50 trains in and out each day, Annesley was handling between 70 and 80, notably the fast fitted freights from the North East to South Wales and the West. There were also the Great Central fish trains still running from Grimsby and Hull to South Wales (Whitland) and Plymouth. These were handled by a variety of mixed traffic locomotives occasionally including the 'Britannias'. It was also not uncommon for WR engines to work freights back to their own region on a balancing trip thus saving a light engine working, which would cause a non-revenue-earning block on the main line.

Parcels traffic too featured on the Great Central, through services running throughout most the day, along with the famous

Great Central newspaper train that was very smartly worked, the empty vans returning from Nottingham the next day attached to the morning Nottingham to Marylebone parcels. The most interesting cross country parcels train was the 06.50 Banbury to York, notably for carrying large quantities of rabbits from the West for consumption in the North. Not surprisingly, it was known to staff as the 'Rabbits'.

Inevitably, the general run down of the Great Central that had begun on the passenger side soon spread to the freight services. Most of the general merchandise and fish trains were either withdrawn totally or transferred to the Midland line via Birmingham to the West. The ASLEF strike of 1953 drove away many freight customers and virtually killed the fish traffic. The new requirements of the coal and power industries, in the shape of the planned 'merry-go-round' systems proposed by the Central Electricity Generating Board and BR, meant that wagon-load traffic would inevitably decline dramatically. It was this decline that dealt the final blow to the Great Central, for it meant the withdrawal of the 'Windcutters' from Annesley to Woodford from June 1965 and, accepting the fact that the passenger service at that time was purely notional, sealed the line's fate.

Above:
A glimpse of the typical Great Central freight train — a 'Modified Class F' travelling at approximately 50mph near Wolfhampcote, bound for Annesley from Woodford on 8 May 1965.   *M. Mitchell*

Below:
Standard Class 9F No 92012 approaches Rugby Central with a down part-fitted freight for Annesley on 22 July 1961.
M. Mensing

Top right:
'9F' 2-10-0 No 92076 passes
Rugby Central with an up freight
from Annesley to Woodford Halse
on 2 April 1963. *D. Smith*

Right:
'B1' 4-6-0 No 61077 at a stand
near Lutterworth on the morning
of Sunday 28 January 1962 as
gangers unload sleepers in
preparation for re-laying track.
M. Mitchell

Below:
On 3 June 1961 BR Standard
Class '9F' 2-10-0 No 92010 is
approaching Ashby Magna from
the north with an up train of steel
products. *M. Mensing*

Above:
'9F' 2-10-0 No 92032 passes Leicester South Goods box with oil tank empties from Abbey Lane Sidings (just north of Leicester Central) to Fawley on 11 June 1965. This was the last booked freight train to run on the Great Central. *H.A. Gamble*

Left:
On 13 June 1962 the crew of 'K3' No 61939, in charge of a Grimsby to Whitland fish train, have halted at Leicester to fill the headlamps with oil. *H. A. Gamble*

Bottom left:
'9F' 2-10-0 No 92033 takes the 16.30 Woodford to Annesley through Belgrave & Birstall station on 15 August 1962. *D. Holmes*

Above:
Two BR '9F' 2-10-0s cross near East Leake with two 'Runners' or 'Windcutters' — the nickname given to the fast 'Modified Class F' unfitted freights. No 92093 approaches the camera with the 16.30 Woodford Halse to Annesley whilst No 92012 storms away with the 17.08 Annesley to Woodford, on 23 July 1962.
D. Holmes

Right:
At East Leake on 4 August 1962 Class O1 2-8-0 No 63817 is passing with the 13.07 Leicester-Annesley freight working.
D. Holmes

Below:
On 14 April 1962 'V2' No 60982 blasts out of Barnston Tunnel with the 05.40 Dringhouses (York) to Bristol Class C freight.
D. Holmes

Above:
'9F' 2-10-0 No 92075 runs through Quorn & Woodhouse with the 17.10 Annesley to Woodford freight on 15 August 1964. *D. Holmes*

Left:
A 'B16' 4-6-0, No 61421 — known to crews as a 'Bloodspitter' — approaches East Leake with a down fitted goods for York Dringhouses on 8 August 1963. *M. Mitchell*

Below:
'Crosti 9F' 2-10-0 No 92021 (with Crosti boiler isolated) is seen south of Loughborough Central with an up freight for Woodford on 18 April 1964. *M. Mitchell*

Right:
Passing East Leake on 29 June 1962 is 'B16' No 61467 with the 16.50 Woodford–York Dringhouses freight.   *D. Holmes*

Below:
'B1' No 61158 races through East Leake with the 06.50 Banbury to York parcels on 7 March 1963. This train was known as 'The Rabbits' due to the large amounts of rabbits carried to be consumed in the North.   *D. Holmes*

Bottom:
'Jubilee' No 45626 *Seychelles* speeds through East Leake with the 10.10 Nottingham–Marylebone parcels on 7 March 1963.   *D. Holmes*

Above:
'K3' No 61893 is going well past Gotham Sidings with the 15.20 Hull–Plymouth fish train on 13 June 1962.   *D. Holmes*

Left:
Shunting Queens Walk to Hotchley Hill empties at Rushcliffe Halt on 3 July 1962 is 'J39' 0-6-0 No 64818.
D. Holmes

Below:
'B1' 4-6-0 No 61002 *Impala* is heading an up fish train near Ruddington at about 16.30 on 19 August 1958.   *T. Boustead*

Above:
'K3' 2-6-0 No 61838 and BR '9F'
2-10-0 No 92010 provide an
unusual combination of motive
power for an up freight passing
Bulwell Common.   *T.G. Hepburn*

Left:
'V2' No 60828 breasts the summit
at Belgrave & Birstall with an up
freight on 23 February
1965.   *J.H. Cooper-Smith*

Below:
The muscular lines of Stanier's
Class 5 design are well defined as
No 45406 heads for Charwelton
with the 11.15 Nottingham–
Marylebone parcels in the
autumn sunlight of 21 November
1964.   *Gerald T. Robinson*

Right:
An awe-inspiring spectacle is
provided by '9F' No 92005 at
speed with an up freight near
Ashby Magna in the crisp autumn
light of 7 December 1963.
M. Mitchell

Below right:
'V2' 2-6-2 No 60963 heads south
on an up freight near Belgrave &
Birstall station on 28 December
1964.   *J.H. Cooper-Smith*

Below far right:
The 06.30 Banbury to
Nottingham parcels at Leicester
Central with '8F' 2-8-0 No 48287
of Birkenhead in charge, on
11 June 1966.   *M. Mitchell*

4

Motive Power

The transfer of the Great Central line to the London Midland Region in 1958 inevitably brought that region's motive power in alongside the Eastern's. Of course, due to its long distance through services, the Great Central was no stranger to 'foreign' motive power, especially from the Western Region. The main traffic concentrations were on the Woodford to Annesley section and the bulk of this traffic consisted of the Annesley to Woodford fast freights, locally known as 'Windcutters'. During the week, Woodford dealt with many up and down services, and Annesley also despatched and received a large number of trains to and from the local Nottinghamshire coalfields.

Numerous cross-country long distance freights were routed via the Great Central line. Daily fitted goods trains ran from Dringhouses (York) to Cardiff, Bristol, Banbury and Woodford; daily fish trains from Hull to Plymouth and Grimsby to

Whitland, and at least five steel trains a day travelled from either Consett or Scunthorpe to South Wales. These formed some of the nine trains a day in each direction that followed the S&MJ route from Woodford to Honeybourne and Gloucester. There was also a daily Dringhouses to Marylebone express freight, and a twice weekly Class C Guinness train from Newcastle to Park Royal also ran.

By 1960, daytime express workings had deteriorated to just three semi-fasts in each direction to or from Nottingham. There was a handful of local trains on various sections of the line and Woodford linked Banbury with about six 'motors' a day. Daily cross-country express workings comprised two York–Swindon night trains and the ubiquitous daytime York–Bournemouth. Summer Saturdays produced various other workings to the south coast resorts; the Sheffield–Hastings, Derby–Ramsgate and Manchester–

Right:
SR 'Schools' class 4-4-0 No 30925 *Cheltenham* at Marylebone on 16 May 1962 after bringing in the 12.15 ex-Nottingham. The service formed part of the locomotive's return journey to the Southern Region after working a rail tour four days earlier from Darlington to Nottingham. *H. A. Gamble*

Eastbourne holiday trains were routed via High Wycombe, whilst the Bradford–Poole, Nottingham–Portsmouth and York–Swansea excursions travelled via Banbury. Finally, night time cheap holiday specials left Marylebone for Scotland at week-ends: the 'Starlights' supplemented the daily night time through trains from Marylebone to Manchester and Liverpool, and the overnight car-sleepers to Glasgow or Perth. Another night train was the Marylebone–Nottingham newspapers, returning next morning to Neasden.

For the 60-wagon 'Windcutters', Annesley was supplied with 28 Class 9F 2-10-0s. Annesley also housed 23 Class O1 and O4 2-8-0s, which served the local coalfields but, on occasion, appeared at Woodford. Also present were some mixed traffic types at this time, namely five 'Crab' 2-6-0s and four 'Black Fives'. Other Midland engines were Nos 41280 and 41320 — the Ivatt Class 2MT 2-6-2 tanks that were used for the workmen's train, known as the Annesley 'Dido', to nearby Bulwell Common. The remainder of this 64 strong allocation was made up of Nos 64739 and 64798 — the last of the depot's long standing 'J39' class locomotives.

Whilst a major duty at Woodford was to service the incoming Annesley '9Fs', it also had its own fleet of 28 WD 2-8-0 freight locomotives. These were used mainly on London-bound freights, on the S&MJ or westbound via Banbury, but also worked to the north to supplement the 'Windcutters'. Woodford's popular 'Green Arrows' had long since moved on, but a strong ex-LNER presence was still evidence in the stud of eight 'B1s', 11 'K3s' and four 'L1' tanks. Its 'B1' No 61028 was named *Umseke* and had previously spent a few years at Leicester Central. Two Midland '3Fs' and 'Mucky Duck' Ivatt 'Moguls' were allocated to Woodford for use on the S&MJ, and four diesel shunters completed the depot's fleet of 59 machines.

Leicester Central housed 21 locos, mainly for passenger duties and local freights. Despite the reduction of passenger services, it still housed three 'V2s', Nos 60815, 60863 and 60890. The rest of the allocation comprised four 'B1s', five 'Standard Fives', two 'L1' 2-6-4 tanks and seven Stanier 2-6-4 tanks. Unfortunately, the 'V2s' were the first of this stud to be expendable when, in November 1961, Nos 60863 and 60890 were put into store and No 60815 was transferred away.

In early 1962, four 'Britannia' Pacifics were allocated to Neasden. Despite the acquisition of these strong locos, the crews were unhappy. Mr R. Clarke, a Neasden fireman, wrote to *Modern Railways,* 'No one in their right mind would enjoy going out on such engines as those in their present condition. Main line dieselisation is the only good thing that could happen to make things better'. Wishful thinking indeed. Dieselisation did arrive, but only on the

63

Above:
On the night of 19 February 1965 a Derby four-car suburban DMU is ready to leave Platform 2 at Marylebone — on this occasion forming the 20.24 parcels service to Aylesbury. *J. Clarke*

Right:
A Derby four-car suburban unit is the formation provided for the 12.25 Nottingham Victoria–Marylebone semi-fast service seen soon after passing Great Missenden on 27 July 1963.
D.F. Chipchase

64

Above:
'Black Five' No 44984 on the
viaducts north of Leicester Central
station with a Rugby-Nottingham
Victoria service on 14 July 1966.
H. A. Gamble

Left:
BR Standard Class 5 No 73004
leaves Lutterworth Station with
the 14.38 Marylebone–
Nottingham Victoria on 22 May
1965.   *M. Mensing*

Below:
'B1' No 61380 is the motive
power for the up 'South
Yorkshireman' seen south of
Tibshelf on 29 September 1959.
M. Mensing

Above:
Rebuilt 'Patriot' No 45529 *Stephenson* leaves Leicester Central with the 11.15 Nottingham–Marylebone parcels on 28 December 1963.
H.A. Gamble

Right:
'9F' 2-10-0 No 92088 at Leicester Central with a Newcastle–Swansea train on 6 August 1960. *Barry O. Hilton*

Below:
'B1' No 61376 approaching Tibshelf station on 29 September 1959 with the 2.10pm Manchester (London Road)–Marylebone. *M. Mensing*

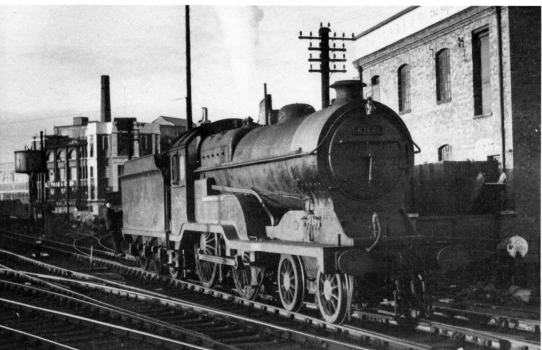

Above:
'V2' No 60856 heads the 08.30 Newcastle–Bournemouth through East Leake on 4 August 1962. D. Holmes

Left:
'Director' 4-4-0 No 62661 *Gerard Powys Dewhurst,* seen on 13 June 1959, will shortly return to Sheffield on the service known as the 'Spitfire' because of its rapid turnround at Leicester. H.A. Gamble

Below:
'Coronation' Class 8P 4-6-2 No 46251 *City of Nottingham* at Leicester Central with the RCTS 'East Midlander' railtour from Nottingham Victoria to Swindon on 9 May 1964. H.A. Gamble

Above:
On 15 August 1964 the 10.48 Eastbourne–Sheffield Victoria relief is powered past Quorn & Woodhouse signalbox by '9F' No 92132.   *D. Holmes*

Right:
At Leicester Central on 28 October 1961 'B1' No 61299 is in charge of the 12.00 to Woodford Halse.   *H.A. Gamble*

Below:
'V2' No 60828 threads the cutting at East Leake on 7 July 1962 with the 11.16 Bournemouth–Newcastle.
D. Holmes

Above:
'Royal Scot' No 46140 *The Kings Royal Rifle Corps* stands outside Leicester shed on 7 May 1961 with 'B1' No 61281.
H.A. Gamble

Right:
Stanier 4MT 2-6-4T No 42556 is active at Leicester Central on 14 October 1962.   *H.A. Gamble*

Below right:
'B1' No 61380 leaves Rugby Central on Sunday 7 September 1958 with an excursion to Hull and Goole, the train having worked in as empty stock from the Leicester direction to start from Rugby.   *M. Mensing*

Above left:
Western Region motive power —
in the shape of modified 'Hall'
No 7919 *Runter Hall* with
Hawksworth tender — is
provided for the 17.20 service to
Woodford Halse at Leicester
Central on 5 May 1961.
H.A. Gamble

Left:
SR 'West Country' class Pacific
No 34102 *Lapford* is admired by
enthusiasts on the platform at
Leciester Central, as it awaits
departure with a FA Cup special
from Southampton to
Nottingham Victoria on 30 march
1963.   *H.A. Gamble*

Below:
'Royal Scot' No 46156 is near
Loughborough with the 09.00
Sheffield Victoria–Bournemouth,
formed of SR Bulleid coaching
stock on 18 July 1964.
Gerald T. Robinson

5

Woodford Halse

A journey between the capital's Marylebone station, the East Midland towns and the North Country necessitated passing through Woodford Halse. Positioned in a fairly southerly part of the Midlands (geographically rather than in the railway sense), much of this Northamptonshire village comprised local stone cottages and urban-style terraced houses in close proximity, imparting to the place something of the appearance of 'Coronation Street' in 'Archers' territory.

Woodford's centrality was a key factor in establishing a railway settlement. The presence of the East & West Junction Railway (later to become the Stratford-upon-Avon & Midland Junction Railway) which offered a possible connection to West Midlands industry, and the proximity of the Great Western Paddington–Birmingham Snow Hill main line (soon connected via the Banbury branch) resulted in Woodford's prominence. The Banbury branch provided important cross-country passenger trains and considerable freight traffic, whilst from the 1950s until the mid-1960s heavy long distance freight travelled over the S&MJ via Byfield between Consett and Scunthorpe in the north and Bristol and South Wales to the west (in fact, the S&MJ's life span was longer than that of the much busier GC line). Woodford railwaymen were particularly involved with these trains.

The village itself was situated some 70 miles from London and approximately twice that distance from Manchester. The coming of the railway had an immense impact on the immediate area as well as on village life. In the 10 years from 1891, Woodford's population had more than doubled to 1,200; in 1931 population rose to 1,700. One hundred and thirty-six Gorton-style terraced houses sprang up 136 miles south of Manchester to house railway families — often comprising newcomers to the area, many from the industrial north. Others of more rustic local stock moved there too, resulting in a community which stood out locally as cosmopolitan yet very tightly knit. Many families became related through marriage, living in what became the largest village in the area — a railway community where the driver was king.

The main obvious gain was in employment. The railway provided an alternative to farm work and locally acquired a status of its own. At a time when few people owned cars, overall-clad railwaymen could be seen cycling to work at any time both within the village as well as to Woodford from Byfield and Eydon while others walked. Local reliance on the line for employment was great from the beginning of the century until rundown in 1965. Local sentiment for railway matters had been conveyed by two one-time shedmasters of the postwar era, both Doncaster trained. Relevant chapters in E.S. Beavor's *Steam Was My Calling* and Richard Hardy's *Steam in the Blood* describe their authors' delight in discovering such feeling in so unlikely a location.

The railway provided a superb service. Pride in fast punctual trains gave the area excellent connections with much of the country's rail network, surely almost unmatched from a village anywhere else. However, much of this traffic was less

Below:
Ex-LMS 2-6-4 Tank No 42178 has just arrived with the 16.13 from Banbury, as 'Black Five' No 45417 departs from Woodford with the 14.38 from Marylebone to Nottingham Victoria on 25 May 1963. *M. Mitchell*

Left:
Fairburn 2-6-4 Tank No 42253 enters Woodford on the 15.35 ex-Aylesbury. The date is 29 August 1962.   *D. Holmes*

profitable than first impressions suggest — a significant proportion consisting of railwaymen and their families using privilege travel tickets.

Much of Woodford's life was rigidly ruled by railway routine. Off-duty railwaymen who supported Leicester City football club travelled by train and could reach the city faster and in greater safety than when travelling by road today. Shoppers used the convenient Woodford–Banbury service to the Oxfordshire town — they still referred to it as the 'Banbury motor' years after it ceased being a motor train. Similarly, they referred to the train running into the 'wooden' platform (originally wooden and formerly used for trains from Byfield and Banbury) after the platform had been rebuilt of concrete in 1956. Secondary school children who had passed the 11-plus examination travelled 10 miles by train to grammar schools in Brackley, to the high school for girls and Magdalen College school for boys. Workers travelled 14 miles to Rugby by train, to work at the BTH factory, but replacement bus services to schools and towns were much slower — the trains were missed.

Just as the railway dominated the senses, so too it dominated conversation. Apart from talk about sport and rural pursuits, the railway dominated conversation on street corners and in hairdressers, pubs and shops. Railwaymen exuded the legend and folklore of the steam locomotive — talking freely of 'rough riders' and 'shy steamers', of the importance of 'filling up the back corners', of the steam-raising qualities of the products of various collieries. Woodford was a railway community embracing the sensuousness of steam. Railwaymen's families regarded such talk as normal, whereas an outsider (whether non-railwayman or person from another village) could find this odd and so feel more of a stranger. Not to be able to converse on railway matters was, for a man in particular, a serious social handicap.

Just as the railway dominated conversation, so it dominated at a physical level. It rose from Eydon parish on the line's ruling gradient of 1 in 176 throughout, except for a short level stretch at the station, only becoming level again near Charwelton water troughs. The railway's presence was betrayed by that symbol of the steam shed,

Below:
No 7900 *St Peters Hall* is at Woodford Station on 29 August 1962 with the 11.16 Bournemouth West to Newcastle. *D. Holmes*

the coaling tower. This LNER-built structure, some 80ft in height, dominated Woodford's skyline for several miles, becoming a local landmark. Steam age atmosphere was conveyed more pungently by the ever present cloud of smoke rising around the shed site.

So much for the atmosphere. Next to some facts gleaned from a 1956 survey, courtesy of Mr J.W. Anscombe JP, former railwayman and local historian. 1956 proves a particularly relevant year to any impression of the line from the mid-1950s until closure a decade later, and the survey consisted of a walk from Eydon parish boundary in the south, along the down side and into Charwelton parish, returning on the up side.

Entering Woodford necessitated passing the site of the disused South Junction. This had been envisaged as a through connection with what became the S&MJ, a hope never properly realised. Further north, beyond Eydon Road bridge, was the yard with loading dock and cattle pens, little used in 1956. The yard housed a concrete building used for storage of cattle and poultry feeds, whilst near the station, an old GC coach was used as lecture room by the ambulance class. Woodford's ambulance classes achieved an enviable success record in competitions against other BR teams.

Station buildings consisted basically of four blocks. The first comprised gentlemen's toilet, cycle and store rooms; the second block contained waiting room and porter's room. Next, until 1954, was the refreshment room — the booking office formed the fourth. Behind the platform entrance/exit was the wooden cabin used by the passenger foreman and guards from which, looking along Station Road, you could see the White Hart Hotel.

No 4 signalbox, sometimes referred to as Woodford Central, controlled movements

at the south end, receiving trains into section from Culworth Junction, Woodford West and Woodford No 3. The latter controlled movements to the old down yard from the down loop and the middle road, and housed the amplifier for the loud speaking apparatus with which the shunting yard was equipped. Two old box van bodies were used for storage of grease and oil.

Among the terraced houses near the river Cherwell were four houses used as hostels for employees needing accommodation. They had been used for visiting crews on lodging turns, a practice discontinued in 1941. By 1956 the locomotive department, not the traffic department, used these — until they met a dramatic end in 1957 when they were burned down. Back along the embankment was the old up yard. There, two roads were used largely for repair of crippled wagons and transhipment of loads of steel, etc, the load having moved in transit.

A little to the north of the Byfield Road bridge, four sidings served the locomotive coal stocking ground — a mobile grab picked coal up to load into wagons. However, at one time, an alternative fuel had been thought likely to be used, though this never happened. In 1947 two oil tanks had been built only to be demolished a decade later when the threat of a coal shortage subsided. Nearby were coaling and drying plants and water tank. Previously, engines had been laboriously coaled by hand — the original structure was retained for emergency use.

Woodford contained a busy carriage and wagon works equipped with a traverser at the north end. On to this wagons were placed, one at a time, and then run sideways into the shops, after which they were run off into one of three roads according to repairs needed, finally leaving from the south end. However, not all repairs were

carried out inside — some were effected outdoors.

Situated north of the sheds was a triangle used to turn engines after the turntable was replaced during World War 2. Adjacent to the sheds close by were the offices of the shedmaster and shed foreman. Running the length of the boilersmiths' shops were the stores, locomotive lamp room and boiler room which housed the boiler used to supply hot water for washing out locomotives; unfortunately Woodford's unsoftened water often proved troublesome. Nearby were the shear legs, rarely used in 1956 — thereabouts was once situated a weighbridge. Between the sheds and wagon shops was situated the former wagon sheet shop, used for storage purposes. To the north in Charwelton parish, was the wartime-built Woodford No 1 signalbox, which controlled traffic entering and leaving the new yards. North of No 1 box were Charwelton troughs and pump, serviced from Woodford.

Returning on the opposite side of the main line, there were offices housing the yardmaster, and telephones for contacting the controllers of various districts — Nottingham, High Wycombe, Birmingham and Gloucester — together with the Post Office telephone exchange at Byfield. A little further south was Woodford No 2 signalbox, sometimes called 'North Loop', which was Woodford's busiest box, controlling movements to and from the up and down sidings and from the sheds and wagon shops. It housed six telephone circuits and the Nottingham control telephone.

Such, in outline, was the railway's presence in 1956. The year was something of a high point in railway activity. New '9Fs', soon to total 45 and whose numbers soon became as old familiar friends rooted to this particular section of line, were making a great impact on the Annesley–Woodford

Above:
'9F' 2-10-0 No 92000 heads a Woodford-bound load of empties up the 1-in-100 gradient between Chacombe Road and Eydon Road on 20 April 1965.
M. Mitchell

Top left:
LMS Class 4F 0-6-0 No 44188 leaves Woodford Halse with an SLS special returning to Birmingham Snow Hill via the S&MJ line on 24 April 1965.
B. Stephenson

Centre left:
Ex-LNER Class L1 Tank runs between Woodford and Banbury with the 17.00 service for Banbury on 14 April 1962. This service was known as the 'Banbury motor'. *M. Mitchell*

Bottom left:
'72XX' 2-8-2 Tank No 7221 stands outside Woodford Shed in the early 1960s. This locomotive was awaiting a freight turn to Banbury and South Wales.
Author's Collection

high-speed, largely loose-coupled freight trains (referred to locally as 'runners'). Unkempt in appearance, but exciting in performance, the speedy 2-10-0s, with their energetic Annesley crews, were often able to perform two round trips between Annesley and Woodford — a distance of 268 miles — in a day. Only a short distance from Woodford's yards, they could be seen speeding along, roaring through Charwelton station and bursting out at Catesby tunnel mouth behind a cloud of smoke and steam. These superb BR-built locomotives had replaced two sound classes of 2-8-0 on the 'runners' — the robust Robinson 'O4s' and competent Thompson 'O1s'.

The 'O4s' usually pulled well against the gradient as witnessed by Charwelton platelayer Vince Smith who remarked how effortlessly they emerged from the tunnel, heading over 50 coal wagons with apparent ease. A Woodford fireman remarked that the 'O4s' were such 'sloggers' that the fireman usually had a chance to sit down! However, some claimed that they were inclined to slip and prone to prime.

Originally, 31 up and 31 down trains were scheduled, at uniform speed and with a maximum load of 50–55 wagons or 60 empties. Such an intense service necessitated a speedy turnaround of engines at Woodford. On arrival Annesley enginemen were relieved by a Woodford crew who took the engine on shed, whilst another Woodford crew brought out a fresh engine for Annesley men to work back. Woodford men were responsible for ash disposal (thus providing a plentiful supply of ash around the pits), and the coaling, watering and preparation of over 30 Annesley engines a day. Generally a little over an hour became the average time taken for locomotive turnaround.

During the mid-1950s, Leicester Central's Gresley Pacifics and 'V2s', with their keen crews, were putting in fine work on the 'Master Cutler' and the 'South Yorkshireman'. Locals claimed that they could tell the time of day by the passage of the named expresses — so accurate was their timekeeping. The distinctive Gresley three-cylinder rhythm with its urgent exhilarating quality could be heard drifting across the fields to neighbouring parishes. This was evidenced by a former Woodford fireman, resident in Byfield, who said that when the air was still, he could hear that three-cylinder sound from near Culworth Junction, through Woodford and Charwelton to somewhere near Catesby tunnel. As such expresses tore through Woodford, windows rattled in the terraced houses at the foot of the embankment, and the ever present sound of shunting would be momentarily drowned. However, Pacifics became rarer after 1957 though the 'V2' class 'Green Arrows' raised the echoes until fairly near closure of the sheds.

Below:
'Austerity' 2-8-0 No 90095 has just pulled up to Woodford West Junction box on the S&MJ line from the GC main line and prepares to run to Newport with the 19.20 train on 11 June 1960.
M. Mitchell

Bottom:
An unidentified 'B1' 4-6-0 approaches Woodford station with a Marylebone to Manchester express on 28 September 1959. The link to the S&MJ line can be seen just above the locomotive.
S. Creer

Although the short-lived named expresses disappeared, freight remained in abundance. The yards contained 33 roads for down traffic. For up traffic there were 11 roads for departures to Banbury, where there was a daily exchange of more than 400 wagons, and 10 for other destinations. During the mid to late 1950s on weekdays, Woodford dealt with 44 northbound arrivals and 43 northbound departures. A total of 42 trains arrived and 47 departed for the south of which 15 ran to or from the Brackley direction. Destinations of down trains included Grimsby, Sheffield, Hull, York and Newcastle, whilst many up trains originated from York.

The S&MJ provided a new route for certain freights — a new road to learn and new experiences. The advantage of this route, to quote from *Trains Illustrated* of December 1959, was 'that it avoided Banbury and the Birmingham areas where the shortage of trainmen was particularly acute'. On Eastern Region initiative it was first used in 1950 — engines used were wartime Riddles 'Austerity' 2-8-0s. Whilst the plodding characteristics of these locomotives were appreciated, their proneness to violent slipping was not. The crews could have problems on two banks — Byfield's gradient of 1 in 107 from Woodford and over two miles of 1 in 98 fron near Aston-le-Walls in the Fenny Compton direction, and Clifford bank in Warwickshire (near Stratford), steeper at 1 in 80. Such stalling created interesting anecdotes. One relates to such a 'steel train' (as these long-distance freights were often referred to locally) getting 'lost' in the section of approximately six miles between Fenny Compton and Byfield. As nothing had been heard of the Woodford crew or train for three hours, a conscientious character, George Holton, set off on foot to investigate. Having

covered less than a mile, he located the train — stalling on this stretch not being uncommon with 'Austerities'. Another Woodford driver, Londoner R.A. Norris, spent an hour with an 'Austerity' slipping on a similar train at Byfield, a few hundred yards adjacent to the ironstone sidings, between Barn Lane and Twistle Bridges. He said that such struggles led to much cursing but considerable overtime claims!

Another Woodford driver and Byfield character, the ubiquitous Dick Hutt, stalled with an 'Austerity' on the Byfield station side of the line's summit (sited near the ironstone sidings). Dick succeeded in climbing the bank by setting back and charging it. At least five minutes for the three quarters of a mile between Byfield station and ironstone sidings was commonplace for an 'Austerity' which has been held in the station loop. From the mid 1950s until 1961, the writer attended the primary school sited a field away from the bank and he can clearly recall the wild wheel-slipping bouts of these locomotives accompanied by volcanic eruptions of smoke and steam which on a bright day could momentarily blot out the sun. Distinctive too was the sound from their snifting valves as they drifted downgrade. The '9Fs', usually the WR double-chimneyed variety, were less prone to such slow starts, as were such Great Western engines as the '28xx' 2-8-0s and 'Halls', which were more common on such freights in the 1960s than in the 1950s.

Trains consisted of semi-finished steel from Scunthorpe and Consett bound for South Wales. They were usually hauled by Woodford, Newport Ebbw Juntion and Cardiff Canton 'Austerities', or '9Fs' shedded at Newport Ebbw Junction and Cardiff Canton. Among the latter, Woodford crews handled BR's last steam locomotive, Class 9F No 92220 *Evening Star,* described as a

Below:
'Modified Hall' No 6982 *Melmerby Hall* leaves Woodford Halse with a freight for the Banbury Line on 18 April 1964. The large blue brick bridge was known as 'Marble Arch'.
P. Riley

satisfactory engine but certainly no better than other '9Fs' for all its fancy finish, and Giesl ejector-fitted No 92250 of which a keen young Woodford fireman remarked that it steamed so well that he felt it would run on dust. Woodford 'Austerities' worked as far as the Newport area.

In the late 1950s there were three or four trains a day from Scunthorpe, as well as two block loads from Consett for the Newport area which from Annesley were pathed into the out-and-home 'runner' service to Woodford. There were nine each way between South Wales and Woodford regularly worked by Woodford men as far as Ashchurch, Broom Junction or Honeybourne. The speed of these trains rarely exceeded 20mph over the S&MJ leading to few wagon casualties — hot axleboxes being a frequent feature of the journey south to Woodford as 'runners'. To illustrate speeds customary over the S&MJ one example will suffice. On 26 April 1963 the writer, in his trainspotting days, left Fenny Compton station on his push-bike at the same time as did No 5928 *Haddon Hall* with its train, and arrived on a road bridge in Byfield as the 'Hall' hove into view half a mile away, slipping slightly on the 1 in 98 bank near Boddington Reservoir.

However, if problems on such banks resulted in sweating and swearing, other benefits accrued for the crews. Much overtime was worked over the S&MJ — something dear to the hearts of quite a few Woodford men. Dick Hutt remarked on the customary slow progress up Clifford bank where the pace was such that one could easily sit on the buffer beam of the locomotive — but if it started to slip then there were problems. R.A. Norris, again with an 'Austerity', hauling a load of 19 'door knockers' (as he called the steel ingots), stalled on Clifford bank, taking at least half a dozen attempts before passing the summit. This section, which normally took less than an hour, had taken over five hours.

Several express freights made the sparks fly over the S&MJ too. Woodford drivers liked to be given a clear road with such freights, as recalled by Byfield signalman and local character Lou Hawkin of Moreton Pinkney. Express freights included the York Dringhouses–Cardiff conveying traffic from North East England to South Wales and advertised by the North Eastern Region as the 'Welshman' and the Dringhouses–Bristol referred to as the 'Bristol'. Often hauled by a 'Hall' over the S&MJ to Woodford they would usually be headed by 'K3s', 'B16s', or 'Green Arrows'. Sometimes it was a case of '9F' haulage over both GC and S&MJ lines — very often a single chimney '9F' on the GC, a double-chimneyed one over the S&MJ. The writer saw the following classes on S&MJ long-distance freights going to or from Woodford, 1955–65:

BR
WD 'Austerity' 2-8-0
'9F' 2-10-0 including No 92220 *Evening Star* and Giesl-fitted No 92250
Standard Class 5 4-6-0

GWR
'Hall'
'28XX' 2-8-0
'72XX' 2-8-2T
'Grange'
'43XX' 2-6-0

LMS
Class 4F 0-6-0 (ex-S&DJR No 44560, 17 April 1961)
Stanier '8F' 2-8-0
Stanier Class 5MT 4-6-0

Doubtless other interested observers could add several more types — the writer has seen a photo of a WR-based BR Standard Class 4MT 4-6-0 on what appears to be such a train in Byfield station.

Below:
Class 24 diesel No D5086 arrives at Woodford with the 16.38 Marylebone–Nottingham on 3 April 1965. *M. Mensing*

Woodford crews occasionally handled types unusual for the line (at least west of Byfield). One experienced Woodford driver could recall having a 'Castle' on a long-distance freight, though with a lighter load than normal — to help it climb the banks, so he said. A keen young fireman could remember a GWR '72xx' 2-8-2 tank engine which he compared with a '28xx' in terms of pulling power but with a more cramped though less draughty cab. The same fireman recalled other GWR tank locomotives on these workings — sometimes a Honeybourne banker would be commandeered. He recalled firing a Hughes-Fowler 'Crab' to Honeybourne and then (because of its unfamiliarity with the relieving crew) firing the 'Crab' back to Woodford. Dick Hutt, with the same fireman, took a Thompson 'B1' — due to a shortage of suitable motive power at Woodford — over the S&MJ. En-route, Dick blew its unfamiliar high-pitched LNER whistle in the region of signalboxes, and was rewarded with some surprised looks.

These S&MJ workings figured surprisingly prominently in Woodford operations of the 1950s and early 1960s. Long distance traffic over the S&MJ west of Woodford totalled many tons — a glance at a map published in *Modern Railways* of September 1962 indicates that at least 50,000 tons per week travelled along this single line. The line was strengthened and new junctions added to handle this traffic. East of Woodford the S&MJ earned less than one tenth of this — less than 5,000 tons per week.

One Woodford working over the S&MJ went no further west than Byfield ironstone sidings — a local pick-up which because of its rambling travels was sometimes called the 'round-the-world'. Such a working might shunt at Woodford West Junction of the S&MJ, set down empties at Byfield ironstone sidings, return with loaded wagons, do more shunting, go on to

Charwelton where more shunting would take place. Also there was a rail-connected ironstone quarry, owned by a different company to the Byfield concern — both quarries worked towards neighbouring Warwickshire. Almost any available steam locomotive that Woodford could lay hands on worked the 'round-the-world'. From the mid-1950s until he saw what seems to have been amongst the last Woodford-worked ironstone train, a mere five loaded wagons handled by BR Standard Class 5 No 73011, on 5 January 1965, the writer noted the following classes hauling this Woodford working:—

BR
(Ex-WD) 'Austerity' 2-8-0
Standard Class 9F 2-10-0
Standard Class 4MT 2-6-0
Standard Class 5MT 4-6-0

LNER
'B1' 4-6-0
'K3' 2-6-0
'K1' 2-6-0
'B16' 4-6-0
'J39' 0-6-0
'O1' 2-8-0
'O4' 2-8-0 (Robinson GC design)

LMS
Fairburn 4MT 2-6-4T
Stanier 4MT 2-6-4T
Ivatt 4MT 2-6-0

Other enthusiasts noted further classes — what a superb illustration of locomotive variety worked from a shed which now seems like a trainspotter's paradise.

Woodford had some slightly unusual workings over the S&MJ, from time to time. These included returning locomotives which had strayed from former LMS sheds, such as Northampton. For example, in an easterly direction from Woodford West, Dick

Below:
'9F' No 92069 backs on to the shed at Woodford on 30 March 1965 to be serviced prior to working north again to Annesley with another 'runner'. *D. Wellington*

Hutt recalled driving a 'Black Five' to Blis-
worth — Dick had worked engines to
Northampton and to Rugby. He also
recalled once driving to Bedford via Olney.
Regarding such ramblings, sometimes locomotives from such Midland line sheds as
Toton might, through some operating
quirk, end up at Woodford. To return these,
often Stanier '8Fs', Woodford men would
haul the dead strangers behind one of their
own locomotives, over the S&MJ to Stratford, where they would pick up a Birmingham Saltley pilotman for the journey to
Saltley via Tyseley. R.A. Norris recalled
doing this from the 1950s when some links
worked west of Woodford West. Woodford
men returned from the West Midlands 'light
engine' to Banbury as they were not allowed
to work a train back to Banbury. The Saltley pilotman was dropped at Banbury whilst
the Woodford crew returned home via the
Banbury branch. Woodford men's last
acquaintance with the S&MJ occurred
when they handled the track lifting train
working to Woodford from an easterly
direction — Woodford men had rarely ven-
tured east along the S&MJ.

Freight movement over the Banbury
branch was also important. Heading towards Banbury Junction heavy freights
needed good brakes south of the 'Marble
Arch', as Woodford men called the blue
brick road overbridge. Uncomfortable
moments were experienced by Woodford
crews with their two Robinson 'Crab' tanks
(originally classed by the LNER as 'L1',
later as 'L3') which could have braking
problems and were inclined to pick up their
wheels and skid descending such gradients
as Chacombe bank. The reverse might apply
against the grade when struggling for
adhesion, though 'Crab' tanks had the

power for hard slogging and were vocifer-
ous about it too. Loud also were 'Austerities' whether blasting upgrade or slipping
ferociously — more than one Woodford
crew stalled with a freight before reaching
the 'Marble Arch', the place reckoned by
Woodford men to signify that the worst of
the climb was behind them.

As well as carrying important freights
and cross-country passenger traffic, the
Banbury branch symbolised something else.
It connected two main lines very proud of
their company origins and the two sheds
with a possessive pride of their own, distinctive even on their own lines. Whilst the
steam age was often characterised by great
camaraderie, there could arise a certain suspicion even between neighbouring sheds on
the same line; when on different lines this
could lead to a certain wariness towards
things 'foreign'. This atmosphere existed
between Banbury on the Western and
Woodford on the Eastern. Woodford crews
found Welsh coal 'foreign' and were wary
of fires on such shared engines as 'Austerities' being clinkered up by Western men's
firing technique, essential with Welsh coal
for which GWR and cosmopolitan train
crews — the cosmopolitan arose with railwaymen transferring from other sheds on
their regions, often with the hope of quicker
promotion. Thus, at Woodford were found
a number of north countrymen, at Banbury
a number of Welshmen.

However, both lines shared a significant
amount of traffic. During the early 1960s,
half the passenger traffic on GC semi-fasts
connected with the 'Banbury motor' at
Woodford. Similarly, south of Rugby, the
daily York–Bournemouth carried twice as
many passengers as the three semi-fasts put
together. By the early 1960s both sheds had

become part of the London Midland Region. Both were united in regarding the Midland as 'foreign'.

In the 1960s the Midland had truly taken over from the Eastern Region. This was evidenced by inclusion of Woodford Halse in the 'Spotlight' series on the back cover of the region's September 1961 magazine. This provides a brief but interesting if inaccurate account by the new 'maroon' masters to whom the line was poor relation. It stated more or less rightly that Woodford was well known to railway enthusiasts for 'its marshalling yard, motive power depot and carriage and wagon repair shops' but gave the village's population as 5,500 — not around 2,000 as it was then and has been ever since. Its rural setting is conveyed when Woodford was stated as being 'situated within an entirely rural area of dairy farming'. Whilst Woodford and surrounding villages were very rural, industry in the local market towns of Daventry and Banbury should not be overlooked. The article further stated that Woodford 'is a typical English country town of mellow stone houses and quiet roads with a profusion of colour in well tended gardens'. Woodford was a village, but was not typical — with its railway contribution — though it possessed some neat gardens and attractive stone houses. Its roads were comparatively quiet — it is not situated on a 'B' road, let alone an 'A' road — though it made up for this by being very much on a main line. Much of its population lived not in attractive 'old Woodford' but inevitably in later houses built very much with railway employees in mind. These were town-type houses — terraced houses to the east of the railway embankment towards Station Road and the large council estate, known locally as the 'new buildings', to the west of the embankment. The article stated that 'the station is a small one' but stressed that 'the marshalling yard area is busy with its daily turn-round of 2,340 wagons and its staff of more than 150. The marshalling yard, motive power depot and station provide work for about 500 local residents, so that Woodford Halse can truly be called a railway town'. Ironically, a mere five years (to the month) saw the last trains run from the 'railway town' which no longer provided employment. This epitomised the end of an era. A mere five years and Woodford had been featured in both the staff's regional magazine as providing work for so many local residents and in a *Sunday Times* article reporting on the death of the railway as a line of communication and important local employer.

It is also interesting to look at what the

Above:
On 29 August 1962 'J39' 0-6-0 No 64727 reverses through Woodford with a permanent way train. *D. Holmes*

local press have said about Woodford. Particularly factual was the *Northampton Mercury & Herald* (August 1954). Headlined 'Woodford Halse — rail centre', underneath followed the words 'Houses 60 locos, has carriage and wagon repair works', 'Woodford is a Northamptonshire railway village' which 'has an importance out of all proportion to its size' and with 'a population of 1,800, is an important centre in the railway world employing 650 men'. The article continued, 'Woodford has four marshalling yards capable of dealing with over 3,500 trucks'. A timely, almost prophetic warning ensued in the last paragraph: 'while everything centres on the railway, many people feel their eggs are all in one basket. Another industry would be a welcome addition, particularly to those who travel daily to factories in Rugby and Banbury'.

Other articles appeared from time to time in other local papers, such as the *Banbury Guardian*. These too stressed how busy the line was and how important it was locally. One article featured no more than a decade after the above, headlined '80 engines a day' with a photo of Shedmaster Coe posed between an 'Austerity' and a 'B1'. The article stated that 'about 270 railway workers were employed there, including 100 drivers and firemen'.

To many railway enthusiasts, particularly those brought up in the steam age, the shed was mecca — a shrine to that God, the steam locomotive. To some who worked there, steam equalled backbreaking, dangerous, dirty and often thankless work. However, during the postwar era and not least the 10 years up to closure of the sheds in 1965, there was a remarkable variety of engines. A few enthusiasts valued Woodford's position — surely some kind of record for such a rural setting. Nevertheless, all too few enthusiasts nationally had either heard of Woodford Halse, or really appreciated the GC line.

Woodford's postwar allocation included engines of the following classes (nicknames in brackets):

MS&L/GCR
'J10'
'J11' ('Pom-Pom')
'L3' ('Crab' tank)
N5

LNER
'B1' ('Springbok')
'B17' ('Footballer')
'J39' ('Standard Pom-Pom')
'K3'
'V2' ('Green Arrow')
Thompson 'L1'
'N2'

LMS
Fairburn 4MT 2-6-4T
Ivatt 4MT 2-6-0
3F 0-6-0
Stanier 5MT 4-6-0
Stanier 8F

BR
Standard Class 5MT 4-6-0
Standard Class 4MT 2-6-0
WD Austerity 2-8-0 ('Aussie')

Interesting are the opinions and experiences of some Woodford locomen regarding their various classes. With enginemens' strong

individuality and conservatism, perhaps compounded by rural suspicion of things 'foreign', here are a few of their opinions. The Great Central spirit of enterprise and enthusiasm is revealed in the interest shown — the following is introduced in the spirit of the adage, 'facts are sacred, but opinions are free'.

MS&L 'J10', No 65158, formerly of Gorton, was allocated for a short while in the late 1950s — its ancient appearance (it pre-dated Woodford sheds) earned it the nickname 'the Rocket' to some railwaymen. Used mostly for pilot duties and classed '2F', it was rarely used on the main line. A similar fate befell several engines whose lineage originated from what many felt was the line's arch enemy — the Midland Railway. Its '3Fs' proved as useless as 'The Rocket'. Neither 'J10' nor Midland '3F' had either the power or versatility of the highly-regarded GC 'J11s' which worked many types of train from the Woodford breakdown train upwards. Woodford housed both slide valve and piston valve variants, including Nos 64331, 64418 and 64428 — many older locomen swore by the 'Pom-Poms' just as they swore at 'The Rocket' and Midland '3Fs'!

Of a distinctive GC design were the 'L3' tanks known as 'Crabs'. In 1950 the first and last numerically, Nos 69050 and 69069, were shedded at Woodford. No 69069, the last surviving 'L3' still being allocated in 1955. They were replaced by Darlington-built Ivatt Class 4MT 2-6-0s Nos 43063 and 43106 on southbound freight workings. Of the two, a Woodford fireman remarked that No 43106 (now preserved on the Severn Valley Railway) steamed and ran better, even when rundown. Another young fireman remarked that with the Ivatts it was necessary to build the fire up at the back of the steeply-inclined grate so as to avoid it being thrown out of the chimney.

'N5s', the product of the line's forbears, seemed competent enough shunters but were replaced by English Electric 350hp diesel shunters (Class 08) Nos 13066–69 by 1955. Initially an employee of the manufacturer guided shed staff, and the shunters were housed in their one road diesel shed adjacent to the steam shed.

Woodford railwaymen appreciated the solid reliability of Robinson's GC designs. The GC's LNER successor also produced some designs which became well liked locally. The 'Springboks' (Thomson 'B1s') were one such class — many crews regarded them as superior to the 'Black Fives' of the rival LMS. Of Woodford's allocation of between half-a-dozen and a dozen from the late 1950s until the early 1960s, Nos 61078

Below:
'K3' 2-6-0 no 61889 heads a northbound freight through Woodford on 29 August 1962. The first three wagons are iron-ore tipplers. *D. Holmes*

and 61271 were kept particularly clean, the latter being regarded as a fine steaming locomotive, whereas Nos 61028 *Umseke* and 61368 were poor. Shedded at Woodford until the early 1960s, crews found the injectors on the 'B1s' (and on other LNER locomotives) much more reliable than those fitted to Stanier's 'Black Fives' and '8Fs'. It was said that a GC line shed fitted a 'Black Five' with injection equipment from a 'B1' with successful results, but that this was removed when the engine went into the shops. Both 'Springboks' and 'Black Fives' rode rough when due for overhaul. However, to Woodford crews the ultimate in roughness were the 'Footballers' ('B17s') — they really could kick! They may have been good looking but they rode rough.

Gresley 'J39s' worked on similar freight turns to the 'Poms-Poms' and were allocated in the early 1960s after the latter had been withdrawn. They replaced the unpopular Midland '3F' and 'J10' 0-6-0s and were quite popular though never eclipsing the 'Pom-Poms'. They had the unfortunate tendency to shed their motion at speed. Not running beyond the early 1960s it fell upon engines such as the 'J39s' to become the stationary boiler — often nicknamed the 'portable' — along the road parallel to the back of the sheds.

The 'K3s' had a mixed reception, being prone to slipping and rough riding, particularly when the motion became worn and they were due for the shops. From the late 1950s, until all had been withdrawn by the end of 1962, Woodford's allocation ranged from half-a-dozen to a dozen. However, it seemed that rundown engines were dumped on the line in general and on Woodford in particular — too often, and with uncanny ease, other shed's 'rough stuff' ended up at Woodford. One or two 'K3s' were so rough that crews were reluctant to handle them — a couple were poor steamers. Some crews found a good 'K3' that ran well: a few of Woodford's earlier allocation, when 'new', were good whilst some of their later allocation were awful.

'L1s' were often found on the 'Banbury motor' and Byfield ironstone trip. From the late 1950s until 1962 Woodford's stalwarts were Nos 67771 and 67789. One of these was involved in an ultimately fatal blowback on the line in Nottinghamshire: the Woodford fireman sustained horrific injuries and that particular 'L1' a tarnished reputation. Such incidents, terrible in themselves, shook the shed and, in a village where a reputation can be quickly earned and very slowly lost, that engine was damned thereafter. Of the two L1s', No 67771 was one of several of its class with a reduced cylinder diameter — one Woodford fireman remarked that No 67771 both steamed and ran particularly well. The 'L1s' enclosed cabs were particularly appreciated in winter and when running bunker first. Several later, rougher 'L1s' from the GE line were fitted with Westinghouse brakes, the irregular thumping sound from these being distinctive. They were thumped by various tools when they proved reluctant to work.

Gresley 'Green Arrows' ('V2s') were almost universally liked locally, being regarded as very capable, competent machines whose only real fault was that the

Below:
On 9 May 1964 at Woodford the driver of 'Coronation' Pacific No 46251 *City of Nottingham* waits impatiently for errant enthusiasts to clear the track and allow him to depart with the R.C.T.S. 'East Midlander'.
P.H. Wells

regulator sometimes blew through. It has been known for one to be positioned apparently safely and with closed regulator after a turn of duty, to have subsequently moved under its own steam. Those regulators tended to exacerbate the problem of slipping when getting a train under way, particularly pronounced with a loose-coupled train. In the words of one Woodford driver, it was 'as though the engine wanted to go but its train didn't'. A free steaming locomotive somewhat prone to priming, a young fireman remarked that when the boiler pressure lifted the safety valves that pressure dropped rapidly and considerably. The same fireman used to love listening to that distinctive Gresley three-cylinder beat from those powerful engines but found frightening the sudden ferocious wheelslips sometimes encountered when travelling at speed upgrade through the damp Catesby tunnel. For a few seconds, seeming more like eternity, all hell would be let loose. Fast — seeming to fly like an arrow — and reliable, Woodford had lost its allocation by the late 1950s. Their warm comfortable cabs were welcome except on the hottest of days. They often visited Woodford with freights from the York direction up until the yards closed.

Of ex-LMS engines Woodford had several classes and, as with LNER types, some received a warmer welcome than others. Fairburn Class 4MT 2-6-4Ts were regarded as rival usurpers of Thompson 'L1s' on such workings as the 'Banbury motor', a service they saw out in 1964. Woodford's Fairburns arrived after closure of Neasden and like 'L1s' they often worked freights and could sometimes be found shunting. One young Woodford shunter preferred 'L1s' to Fairburns as they were less liable to slip. However, they were less powerful than the Thompson locomotives and were not so fast off the mark.

Ivatt Class 4MT 2-6-0s were the forebears of a BR Standard design several of which were allocated in the early 1960s. Both classes avoided notoriety, and both had more reliable injectors than 'Black Fives' and Stanier '8Fs'. As with the 'Ivatt 4s' so too with BR Class 4 'Moguls' it was fatal to build up an even fire; far wiser to put plenty of coal in the 'back corners'.

Woodford possessed an unusual distinction regarding Class 5 motive power in the early 1960s. During this transitional phase, Woodford housed LNER, BR and LMS Class 5s whilst Woodford crews were conversant with GWR Class 5s — the 'Halls', 'Granges' and 'Manors'. They found that the 'Black Fives' could run well, still steaming with indifferent firing, but many preferred the 'Springboks'. However, some said that the 'Springboks' became rougher at speed than the 'Black Fives'. Other crews preferred the BR development from the 'Black Five' — the Standard Class 5s had better injectors and seemed to run easier and faster than the LMS engines. Woodford was one shed which took to the Standard Class 5s and was sorry to see them replaced by 'Black Fives' — perhaps old loyalties lingered and their driving wheel diameter and motion being more akin to that of the 'Springboks' made Woodford men feel more at home. Whilst Standard Class 5s usually steamed well, No 73000 was regarded as particularly free-steaming, in contrast to another particularly poor one (the latter was also distinguishable by having a different style of numerals on its pressure gauge). One feature of the Standard Class 5s when in the hands of some extrovert crews was the frequency with which they delighted in blowing the chime whistle.

Below:
'B1' No 61008 is running tender first as it hauls the 17.08 service to Banbury out of Woodford Halse on 23 May 1959.
M. Mitchell

This evocative sound could often be heard punctuating other railway and rural sounds, most hauntingly during winter's stillness or in the dead of night.

Stanier '8Fs' replaced WD 'Austerities'. The Stanier '8Fs' were nicknamed 'Midland 8s', the 'Austerities' 'Aussies'. During the early 1960s a line of at least 10 'Austerities' was stored alongside the coal heap between the coaling tower and Byfield Road bridge. Always rough riding, surely there was a parallel between the riding of these machines and the rock 'n' roll era! One of these 'shake, rattle and roll' machines had apt graffitti applied to its smokebox door — 'Duane Eddie'. Although the rugged WD design was a simplified derivation of the Stanier engine, Woodford received Stanier '8Fs' as replacements. Comparisons, based on the comments of various crews, are interesting — the WDs rode rougher than the less austere Stanier '8Fs' but had more reliable injectors; the brakes on some WDs seemed slack whilst those on Stanier '8Fs' were good. Both when in reasonable order, could steam and pull well, with the Stanier '8Fs' being faster. To reduce the rough riding of the WDs, several had the drawbar between engine and tender shortened by Woodford fitters resulting in a marked improvement. As with all classes, some steamed and ran better than others — from the late 1950s until the early 1960s Woodford was well acquainted with them, having more than a score.

Woodford's central position resulted in many classes working to the sheds. Classes handled by Woodford crews after World War 2 included:

GC
'O4' ('Tiny')
'Q4' ('Old fashioned lady)

LNER
'A3'
'K2'
'B16'
'O2' ('Tango')
'K1'

BR
Britannia
'9F'
4MT 4-6-0

Ex-LMS
Hughes-Fowler 'Crab'
'Jubilee'
'Scot'

Ex-GWR
'28XX'

In addition, more classes visited — these might be in the hands of crews from other sheds. For example, Neasden worked Southern 'Schools' No 30925 *Cheltenham* (now preserved) to Woodford on the 6.10pm from Marylebone in May 1962. Although, due to lack of light, the writer was unable to photograph this visitor, he managed to record 32 different classes on the line locally in the five years from 1962 to 1966. Some of these included preserved visitors on enthusiast specials providing a contrast with lines of withdrawn locomotives being towed to northern scrapyards. Army 'J94' 0-6-0STs could be seen either en route from one army depot to another or, from Barby camp, receiving an 'X-day' (basic check-over) at the sheds.

Although, apart from diesel shunters, Woodford was an all steam, shed, the following types of 'modern traction' were noted from 1961 to 1966.

Diesels
LMS Co-Co (built 1947)
Class 24
Class 25
Class 31
Class 35 'Hymek'
Class 37
Class 40
Class 47

Gas Turbine
GT3

Local enthusiasts could add more classes. From 1962 one regular diesel working was for a Sheffield Darnall diesel to work as far as Banbury on the York–Bournemouth, usually a problem-prone Class 31, 37 or 47. Diesel movements of note included brand new rodless 'O8s' in goods trains hauled south and west of Woodford to homes in Western sheds. Class 37s ran light or coupled together to their first homes on the Western. 'Hymeks' ran light from their Beyer-Peacock birthplace in Gorton (near to the GC Gorton tank works area). The writer noted new D7018 passing light engine on 10 January 1962 — this diesel-hydraulic is now preserved at Didcot. The hydraulics, including 'Westerns', could be heard in the quiet of evening on northbound trains from the Western Region. D7023 was observed leaving the station on a York-bound train, on the fateful evening of 3 September 1966.

Woodford's Eastern shedcode, 38E, became extinct when the Midland Region took over. Woodford became 2F in the Rugby area for several years from the late 1950s, initially alongside such sheds as Warwick, Coventry and Northampton.

Around 1963 further changes occurred — shedcode 2F was transferred to Bescot in the West Midlands, whilst Banbury became 2D, transferred from the former Western Region Wolverhampton Stafford Road area to Birmingham Tyseley. At this time Woodford, shedcode 1G, fell under the London Willesden area alongside sheds such as Marylebone, Rugby and Northampton. Latterly, in common with some engines from other sheds, some Woodford locomotives had their shedcodes painted on their smokebox doors — what with souvenir hunters collecting the metal shedplates and the probable rarity of these new increasingly strange codes, this practice increased. During BR's run-down of steam, some engines, including 'Black Fives', could be seen minus shedplate but with shed name, such as Annesley, painted on the bufferbeam. This, at least, was reminiscent of LNER practice.

The 1G shedcode was particularly short-lived. Engines whose numbers began with 4 almost totally colonised the shed; those beginning with 6, once predominant, became an endangered species. Engine failures increased, and both shed and locomotives became increasingly run-down; in June 1965 the end came. On the evening of Friday 11 June four locomotives were observed there: one 'Black Five', two Stanier '8Fs' and one Fairburn tank. The following day saw five: 'Black Fives' Nos 44814 and 44835, Stanier '8Fs' Nos 48002 and 48121 and Fairburn tank No 42082. Local railwaymen said that No 44814 was the last locomotive to leave — thus no LNER or even BR engine was present during the shed's dying days. On the following Monday the shed was deserted, except for a few old wagons. From then until closure of the line a little over a year later, less than a dozen enginemen booked on at the station to crew Banbury 'Black Fives' sup-

plied for the southern end of the line.

Little need be said of the devious destruction of this once great line. The 'Black Fives' frequently failed with injector trouble, and attained an increasingly black reputation and grime-encrusted appearance. Of this period E.J.S. Gadsden wrote in the November 1966 *Railway World* 'already the track has been lifted and only the running lines and siding remain, the buildings stand empty, their windows broken and signalboxes are shut'. What could never happen there, had — with devastating speed and dramatic effect. Only a decade earlier Woodford had been dominated by the steam locomotive — from the sleek, speedy Gresley Pacifics to the pounding, plodding Austerity 2-8-0s.

Until the fateful year of 1965, over half of Woodford's workforce was employed on the railway, and many railwaymen had started their working lives believing they had a job for life. However, in 1965 the yards, then the sheds, shut. Woodford's future looked bleak — the process from 'runners' to run-down had been remarkably rapid. Surrounding villages noticed the loss also, though to a lesser extent — for Byfield the railway at Woodford had been the largest single employer. Additionally, some years before run-down, several young firemen, often teenagers, had been drawn from surrounding (but not neighbouring) villages, attracted by high pay. Meanwhile, in postwar years, a greater proportion of the youth from Woodford's railway families had been attracted by the more regular hours of factory work — they had exchanged the sound of locomotive whistles for that of the factory hooter.

Woodford's history is nothing if not unusual — its railway run-down as rapid as its volcanic rise — but even structures fought valiantly as the army found when

Below:
Woodford MPD on 2 March 1963. On shed are (left to right) 'Jubilee' No 45567 *South Australia*, Churchward 2-6-0 No 6345, Stanier Class 5 No 44688 and 'V2s' Nos 60941 and 60961. *L. Sandler*

attempting to effect demolition, making the national news in the process. Near the station in 1967, a derailed tracklifting train had to be lifted back on to the track by a steam breakdown crane. The locals' possessive pride in the railway was often replaced by a critical, sometimes downright hostile attitude to things railway, resulting from such speedy deprivation. The loss was deeply disturbing yet strangely moving. A few years earlier Woodford's inhabitants, who had been full of railway talk, suddenly hated talking of the railway. However, railway terminology and thinking survives to this day. For example, throughout the chapter the term 'Woodford railwaymen' embraces the definition as understood by both railwaymen and enthusiasts, namely those who were based at Woodford. They need neither have originated at nor even have lived in Woodford. By contrast, to most non-railway-orientated people locally, Woodford men would simply refer to men from Woodford (regardless of any involvement with the railway).

Ironically, many former railwaymen found employment in industries allied to rail's rival, road transport. The raucous echo from Commer two-stroke lorries transporting motor components from Coventry to a local export packing station replaced rhythmic reverberations from 'Green Arrows' around Charwelton and the sound of 'Austerities' blasting up grade around Byfield. Similarly, the sound of a 'Springbok' accelerating briskly away from Charwelton with a local passenger train was replaced by the booming two-stroke sound of a Taylor's bus on a local shoppers or works run from Daventry or Rugby. The 'Banbury motor' became motorised with a railway replacement bus service between Woodford and Banbury, initially operated by Owen's of Upper Boddington and later

by its successor, Geoff Amos coaches of Eydon. Instead of handling such locomotives, former railwaymen travelled in buses to the packing station or commuted to factories in Daventry, Leamington and Coventry. Banbury, Rugby and Northampton provided some railway work — some former railwaymen learned modern traction and 'new roads' on transferring to bases in those towns. The Rugby BTH workers' early morning train, which on occasions was powered by such comparative rarities as 'K2s', had been replaced by a bus several years prior to closure.

Former railwaymen found themselves in a very different world. The self-contained community had disintegrated and local market towns were changing too. Big city brashness contrasted with rural reticence — Daventry became a Birmingham overspill development, Banbury is a London overspill town. However, Woodford seems well known locally on two contrasting counts. It has a good selection of shops in Station Road (for a village of its size) and, according to the results of a survey in a local paper several years ago, a very high rate of family break-up and divorce.

Woodford never quite became the 'ghost town' feared, although haunted by its railway past. Even so, men barely middle-aged when the line was alive are now pensioners, and many of the characters have passed on. Woodford's future is envisaged in Northamptonshire's County Plan as that of 'rural service centre'. The former BR Staff Association is now a special club and small industrial units have been constructed north of the Byfield Road bridge site. Woodford has lost its secondary modern school but looks set to gain an estate of over one hundred private houses.

Woodford might then be summed up as a peculiar place with a fascinating past — perhaps explained in part by the fact that both railway and farming communities tend to be set apart. To rail enthusiast MP Robert Adley it was 'a strange isolated community whose existence was inextricably linked with the railway'. Edwin Allen of Byfield could remember Woodford before the opening. He worked briefly in the sheds, watched some of the last trains (including those driven by brother Sam), and saw the village after its loss.

More quotes from local papers are of interest. The station had been hewn apart against a chillingly apt winter landscape in December 1967 — the site is now used as winter quarters for fairground folk. Seventy-five acres of shale resulted from lifting of the line, recalled in such headlines as 'Ballast an eyesore at Woodford'

(November 1975), 'How can Woodford get over its hump?' (October 1971), 'Barrier to be a link' (April 1976). Local papers were full of such phrases as 'Those wasted acres are to be reclaimed', referring to purchase from BR of 61 acres and the acquisition of an industrial estate of about six acres (January 1979); 'New hope for a "ghost" town — full steam ahead for Woodford revival plan'. The embankment was 'a derelict legacy from a thriving rail centre. (The *Rugby Advertiser*, July 1976). The *Daventry Weekly Express* reported in August 1976 that, at a meeting, a speaker felt that 'the appearance of the railway bank had worsened considerably of late and was now a dumping ground for old cars and other rubbish'. The same paper had reported that as the last freight 'wailed its goodbye' in 1965, 'to the railway village of Woodford Halse', it concluded, 'It was good-bye to an era. The end of a way of life'.

Two quotes, one humorous and one serious, concerned a 'time warp' and possible development. The amusing item appeared in the *Daventry Weekly Express* in January 1972 headlined 'The Yellowed Pages'. Approximately six years after closure of the line the Northampton yellow pages telephone directory still contained the entry: 'Woodford Halse — passenger, goods and yardmaster: Byfield 402'. Meanwhile, a possible route for the proposed M40 Oxford–Birmingham motorway was discussed under the headline 'Old rail line for M-way?' in the *Coventry Evening Telegraph* (November 1971). It has been suggested that the M40 follow at least part of the former line somewhere north of Aylesbury to south of Rugby. From main line to motorway?

For much of the world, the 1960s symbolised optimism — a carefree, booming time. To Woodford the 1960s spelt growing pessimism, a worrying time fraught with fear of almost panic proportions, a period of gloom and doom. The decade which proclaimed life and peace worldwide spelt death to the line and disruption to Woodford. However in the mid-1970s a new group was formed with the aim of salvaging at least a little of what might be left from the line's local past. This was the Great Central Railway Enthusiasts' Association (Woodford Halse). Initially, many members were former railwaymen but in the ensuing decade several senior 'founding fathers' have passed away including former Carriage & Wagon shop Foreman Mr Reg Adams and driver Dick Hutt who played a prominent part in driving the last trains. Several were interviewed on the station site, in 1976, for BBC *Nationwide*.

Alas, too little was saved — items of local railwayana are few and far between. The Association has saved a few, and some photographs which would otherwise have been destroyed. The majority of open meetings, of necessity, concern themselves with other lines as well. Thus, 10 years after its birth the Association resembles other railway societies whilst retaining a bias towards the line, railways locally, and the steam age in general.

The average age of members is now younger and it draws its membership from several local towns as well as from further afield. The overall aim is to preserve some memory of the line to prevent Woodford becoming a forgotten place in a forgotten area on a forgotten line. The Association was featured in the *Daventry Weekly Express* of 25 September 1981, in an article headlined 'Steam — it's in our blood', below which was a feature headed 'End of an era — but silence hangs uneasily over a village'. This surely sums up the brooding intensity of the Woodford of today.

To some steam age enthusiasts Woodford typified a railway community — a place to which people travelled. To a generation which has come of age locally Woodford symbolises a kind of commuter village — a place from which people travel. To past generations of railwaymen, enthusiasts and locals it would have been impossible to imagine Woodford without steam locomotives, let alone a working railway.

In a village where people can be earthy of expression, forceful of feeling, and earnest in argument, who is blamed for the loss of the line? Opinions vary — several culprits emerge. Factors blamed include, devious destructive 'Midlandisation', nationalisation, the Marples-Beeching regimes, and vested road transport interests. However, it must be acknowledged that even if the line had survived, Woodford's yards and sheds would have been at best much reduced in an age of air-braked block trains, containerisation and diesel traction.

The future of Woodford today lies more in its surrounding area, which has been described in the past as unmitigated, forgotten Midlands. With expanionist pressures from the nearest large urban areas — the West Midlands conurbation and the Greater London area, and the increasing suburbanisation of village life, however, local towns and villages are becoming part of a relatively rural south Midlands meeting place between such urban areas with their increasingly insistent needs for more housing and industry for this well-placed area of Central England. Just as the past was fascinating, the future could prove interesting, and less of a one-track existence.

6
Reasons For Closure

The first paragraph of the Beeching Report merely confirmed the suspicions of the British Transport Commission when it had initially taken over the railway companies after World War 2. It concluded with a statement made by the Prime Minister speaking in the House of Commons on 10 March 1960:

'First the industry must be of a size and pattern suited to modern conditions and prospects. In particular, the railway system must be remodelled to meet current needs and the modernisation plan must be adapted to this new shape.'

Of course, the network was still far too large in 1960 for the traffic volumes that were available. Even when the major centre-to-centre flows were examined, it was found that with modern signalling and diesel or electric traction more traffic could be handled with less resources; in effect, the capacity of routes could be vastly increased. Considerable savings in manpower would result and long distance passenger and freight services could easily be diverted from one trunk route to another.

The Beeching Report also marked the first occasion on which the needs of the railway industry had been looked at from a national viewpoint, (though the London Midland Region's own strategists had recognised that routes needed rationalising and indeed had started on the Great Central almost immediately on its transfer to the region). Before the instigation of this national approach, the Regions had competed against each other as they had done in the days of the 'Big Four'. The main factor to emerge out of all of this research was that Britain had to have (and still has to have) a national railway system responsive to the needs of the customer who ultimately pays the wages. Governments of all parties had realised that the huge losses BR would continue to make if left alone would not only be disasterous for the railway industry itself, but also for the nation, which could no longer afford to live beyond its

means. The upshot of Beeching was that routes would be developed between the major centres of Britain which catered both for existing traffic requirements and those that were likely to exist in the future. It has left us with the relatively successful railway of today.

The question to be asked after Beeching was which routes would be retained? The South Yorkshire and East Midlands areas were served equally by the Midland — the longer-established route — and the Great Central London extension which had arrived on the scene in 1899 and was the last main line to be built up to the capital. It had been obvious to many railwaymen that only one route to these areas was justified: in fact, on economic grounds, it can be argued that the Great Central line should never have been built. Had the wider scheme of the link to the Channel ports materialised, the Great Central would have formed a far more important route, but with just a terminus in London, it was a far less attractive proposition. Indeed, the Great Central Railway never paid a dividend on the ordinary stock it had issued when the line was first built. Financial results were always poor and a major reason was the sparsely populated area the line passed through between Rugby and Aylesbury. The line also had two routes in to London — one via the Metropolitan through Amersham and Rickmansworth to Marylebone, and the other via Grendon Underwood Junction (near Calvert) which ran through Ashendon, High Wycombe and Princes Risborough and thence to Neasden and Marylebone. Though joint lines, the availability of two routes doubled maintenance requirements, and train working costs became higher as a result. It also created problems with the Western Region on the High Wycombe route which saw Great Central trains very much as 'foreign'.

In LNER days, the Great Central had managed to live off the fat of the successful East Coast route, and for good measure the competition with the Midland or LMS was good for LNER prestige. It also fed valuable tonnages of freight from the South Midlands and South West via Woodford Halse up to the Nottingham and Sheffield areas and ultimate the rest of the LNER system. This continued into Eastern Region days when the Great Central was still very busy with freight. However, the vast majority of this traffic left or joined the system at Woodford, leaving the few expresses and locals dominating the southern section towards Aylesbury and the commuter belt, although it must be said that these services were very smartly operated.

However, the long distance expresses and cross country services could easily be diverted as could many 'stoppers' on the Sheffield, Nottingham, Leicester and Rugby services. Most of the other smaller stations served small communities and were prime targets for closure. Indeed by 1963 only around 5,000 passengers per week used the Great Central between Aylesbury and Rugby. The Rugby to Nottingham service did little better with only some 10,000 per week. This was of course reflected in receipts; with the exception of Marylebone, only Leicester Central, Nottingham Victoria and Aylesbury stations were earning over £25,000 per year. Freight services too were easily transferrable, the through Northeast to South West trains being re-routed via Birmingham and even the Annes-

ley to Woodford coal trains were threatened by changes in the power industry.

Why was the Great Central a target? Passing through very sparsely populated areas, the London Extension was built to provide a fast run south to London from the Great Central homeland in the North and, unlike the Midland which operated its own cross country services, the Great Central only had the Woodford to Banbury link to provide additional passenger traffic. Further to the North, the Great Northern and Great Central Nottingham to Derby service (from Grantham) went nowhere near the important centre of Derby Midland with its through connections to most parts of Britain. The other critical factors in deciding the Great Central's ultimate destiny were the placing of the power stations in Britain in relation to the coalfields, and the future envisaged for rail-borne coal traffic generally. The Woodford to Annesley service, the life blood of the postwar Great Central, was formed of the traditional 'wagon load' operating method. The new requirement for coal was to move away from wagon load traffic in favour of the 'merry-go-round' system of moving coal directly from pit to power station in block trains. The Midland routes were entwined around the essential waters of the river Trent and this is of course where the modern power stations were built. This new practice of coal carrying virtually eliminated the main carryings of the Great Central and left it without one of its most important flows.

However, the Great Central Railway had advantages over the Midland when it came to express passenger operation. The line was brilliantly engineered for fast running — indeed, the minimum radius of curves was one mile, eased in one case only to 60 chains. Also, between Aylesbury and Rugby there was a maximum gradient of 1 in 176 and the line tended to cut through hills in deep cuttings and over valleys on high embankments. Despite having to share tracks with the Metropolitan electrics south of Rickmansworth (before the service was extended to Amersham), the Great Central line could have provided a very fast run to the East Midlands, when compared with the Midland. Both lines suffered from mining subsidence north of Nottingham, but more attention had been given to repairing the Midland, leaving the Great Central services plagued with speed restrictions.

Another major consideration was that the Great Central proved to be a problem to operate under Regional control until a clear decision was taken to give it to the London Midland Region, which geographically made more sense. Serving the same places as the Midland route, and already running a 'secondary' service from 1960, the Great Central became a financial burden — to an even greater extent than it had been since the start of nationalisation, and indeed as it had been to the LNER. The best initial

Below:
Another factor that caused the LMR to close the GC was that the ex-LNER line did not fit into the ex-Midland lines it ran, such as Norwich-Birmingham and Nottingham-Derby-Crewe. It was certainly superior to the Midland for fast running as ably demonstrated by Standard Class 9F 2-10-0 No 92093 storms past Ashby Magna station with an up freight for Woodford on 21 September 1961.
M. Mensing

Bottom:
'A3' Pacific No 60049 *Galtee More* arrives at Rugby Central with the 07.47 Marylebone to Leicester Central semi-fast service on 7 November 1956.
M. Mensing

compromise was to leave it to one region to operate and, due to its entanglement with other routes, give the marketing and engineering rights to the London Midland Region from Ashendon and Quainton as far as Chesterfield, and give them south of these points to Marylebone via Princes Risborough (including Neasden depot) to the Western Region, thus leaving the Rickmansworth and Harrow route to the London Transport Executive which ran as 'prime user' on that section.

Not surprisingly the Regions, confused enough at having to try to operate as one railway since nationalisation, found the arrangements on the Great Central railway very difficult. Perhaps it was more confusing to the railway staff at the southern end of the route who had been LNER and were suddenly Western men with any promotions only to Western sheds. From the commercial point of view, the same problems occurred with considerable liaison becoming necessary between York and Paddington, thus creating extra administration and wasted time in getting things done.

Mounting losses and the redrawing of the regional areas saw the Great Central railway rationalisation start. The Eastern and London Midland Regions had no case for retention of the line as a major route, and thus the Great Central was earmarked for closure even before publication of the Beeching Report. Beeching confirmed the closure had to take place in Point No 1 of his 15 conclusions which recommended 'discontinuation of many stopping passenger services' ie removal of the only Great Central passenger service left (save the York–Bournemouth), after the freights had been earmarked for withdrawal. On 3 September 1966 the recommendation was implemented.

Top left:
'K3/2' No 61950 heads an up fast fish train south from Rugby Central on Whit Monday 26 May 1958. *M. Mensing*

Centre left:
'V2' 2-6-2 No 60854 rests at Marylebone after arrival with the 'Master Cutler' from Sheffield Victoria on 28 September 1957. *C. Boocock*

Bottom left:
'Britannia' 4-6-2 No 70046 (formerly *Anzac*) and BR Standard Class 5 No 73048 prepare to leave Marylebone with the 14.38 to Nottingham on 27 October 1965. *H.N. James*

Above:
'Britannia' 4-6-2 No 70054 (formerly *Dornoch Firth*) is seen passing the remains of Charwelton station on 2 October 1965 with the 14.38 Marylebone–Nottingham.
M. Mensing

Centre right:
On 1 September 1966, two days before the end, 'Black Five' No 44858 enters Nottingham Victoria with the stock for the 17.15 service to Marylebone.
R. Siviter

Right:
'Black Five' No 44835 stands at Nottingham Victoria with a Marylebone to Preston parcels train on the night of 18 February 1965. This service was diverted to the West Coast main line on 1 March 1965. *J. Clarke*

7

The Last Day

The Great Central Railway had begun to die long before its actual exlcution in September 1966. Of all the lines that were cut under the 'Beeching axe' most disappeared with the familiar last day special and much local agony but not too much national controversy. However, one or two lines which were followed with great affection by many people became the subject of adulation and deep-set mourning. The mid 1960s had seen the demise of the much-loved Somerset & Dorset with the complete removal of a long line through beautiful countryside. The Great Central also had its many followers and the writing was on the wall from the time at which British Rail decided to concentrate services from Nottingham and Leicester through Kettering into St Pancras. It was ironic that the last main line built and indeed the best engineered was the one that was to close. The rot had set in long before with the traditional reduction in services, the imposition of speed restrictions, the transfer away of items of rolling stock and re-routeing of peak through trains. As diesels took over from steam engines in other parts of the country, the displaced locomotives were gradually transferred to depots such as Colwick, Woodford Halse and Banbury. Woodford, with its mass of engine running lines now deserted was a forlorn sight. To see the magnificent 'Britannia' Pacifics reduced to pulling four coaches in the most appalling condition was too much for many people and they turned their backs on the Great Central. For the dedicated follower of this great line the last few months became almost ritualistic. Much of the adulation was centred around the trains which ran at 38min past the even hour from Marylebone to Nottingham — usually hauled by a very grimy 'Black Five'. On many occasions drivers had a job to get up the bank to Harrow-on-the-Hill let alone plod their way through Aylesbury and on to Nottingham. For many of these locomotives the cutter's torch would be a merciful release, for how much longer could they go on in the condition they were in? There are many horrendous stories from the last days of the Great Central from the train crews involved, mainly men reaching their retirement, based at Marylebone, Colwick and Banbury. One such is that on a dim and dismal night during the last few weeks a driver had to stop his engine at a signal

Right:
The last GC main line steam train at Marylebone. No 44984 waits to depart with the 22.45 express to Manchester on 3 September 1966. *E.J.S. Gadsden*

in order to get out and clean the aspect because he just could not see whether it was red or green. Maintenance was almost non-existent, and the line was plagued by speed restrictions throughout its length. The last week was too much for many people; four-car trains to Nottingham were packed to capacity in both directions and the loyal many chased the paper trains at night and logged every movement up and down the line. The last day of operation was 3 September 1966 and apart from the one or two local booked services on that day, the actual last train rites were entrusted to a special organised by the Locomotive Club of Great Britain, which upset many of the faithful by not only originating from Waterloo but having 'Merchant Navy' Pacific No 35030 *Elder Dempster Lines* as motive power from Waterloo to Nottingham and back to Marylebone. The only consolation on this trip was the fact that two immaculate 'B1s' were rostered to run from Nottingham north through Sheffield and back again. The Great Central Rail Tour, as it was known, left on a lovely bright sunny morning and negotiated the West London suburbs through the traditional route to Kew and then had to effect a complicated shunt movement at Neasden in order to gain access to the main Great Central Line. Participants on the tour saw the well known figure of Brian Stephenson, camera poised, photographing the train in the Rickmansworth area, and this picture has become part of the history of the ending of steam on British Railways.

The first stop for photography and water was at Aylesbury where a considerable crowd had gathered on the platform and lineside to see what was in fact for them a very rare locomotive event; rare not only in that the motive power was unusual for that area but indeed it was the first time for many years that a clean locomotive had been seen in the vicinity. The journey to Nottingham was fairly uneventful and included another photo stop at Loughborough. At Nottingham there was no sign of the 'B1s' but they eventually arrived, were turned and watered and then took the train off on its northbound meanderings through old Great Central freight and passenger lines. The arrival back at Nottingham Victoria was in the late afternoon when the murk was really setting in. Nottingham Victoria, with its tunnels at each end, was murky at the best of times but the dimness of the evening and the sadness of the occasion gave it an air of gloom that was unprecedented in the history of the station. The well loved Inspector from Feltham on the Southern Region, Arthur Jupp, was on the footplate of the 'Merchant Navy' which backed on from Colwick depot and was crewed by Marylebone men. It was a touching finale that the driver was on his last run before not only redundancy but retirement. Ted Kitcher, the loveable Trains Inspector who was the feature of the many 'Farewell to Steam' specials, was also on board the train. From the moment the 'Merchant Navy' left Nottingham, everybody knew this was the beginning of the end of an era. The farce of the speed restrictions that had been imposed on the line became apparent when the 'Merchant Navy' and her coaches maintained a steady 70mph over the length of the line without any noticeably rough riding.

By this time it was pitch dark and the only glimpse one had from the train of the

Below:
No 44984 with the last 17.15 Nottingham Victoria to Marylebone passing the site of Culworth station on 3 September 1966. *M. Mensing*

last day of the Great Central was of the gas lights still burning on the country stations with groups of people standing to pay their last respects. The arrival at Marylebone at approximately 10pm became the usual sad occasion, with candles lit on the buffer beam of the locomotive. The most touching remembrance of this particular run was the tribute paid by Inspector Arthur Jupp to the driver and fireman whose last run this was. They had demonstrated a tremendous level of railway operating experience when it is considered that they had never set eyes on, let alone driven, a 'Merchant Navy', the locomotive had performed perfectly throughout the run. Late that evening she shunted the empty stock backwards out of Marylebone, ran round the train and hauled the empty stock back via Neasden to Clapham Junction with the locomotive returning to Nine Elms. For Marylebone and points north this was the end, no longer would trains run between Aylesbury and Rugby. Various sections of the line were left to operate in truncated form, but 3 September 1966 saw the last through running.

Many of the faithful had decided to stay with conventional rolling stock and motive power for the last day. There were many interpretations as to what was actually to be the last service train, but it was generally accepted that the 5.15pm Nottingham to Marylebone and the 10.45pm Marylebone to Manchester were to be accorded the due honours. Many people joined this train — an eight-coach mixture of various carriages running to a weight of about 280 tons — which was hauled by 'Black Five' No 44984 from Colwick. Driver Tom Pavey from the ill-fated Woodford Halse depot was at the controls of the loco which, despite a terrible external appearance, was in remarkably fine engineering fettle. Speeds in the mid-60s were maintained as far south as Rugby Central. It was also very touching that Driver Pavey's wife was also present en route amongst the large crowds. Water was taken en route, which was an added precaution in case there was technical trouble in that the locomotive would not reach London. This particular train maintained strict observance of the speed restrictions that were imposed all over the line but did manage to achieve a maximum speed of 71mph in the Calvert area. Aylesbury again provided a large crowd of people who were there to pay their respects and with the train only leaving a few seconds late it was very clear that this train if no other was going to be on time into Marylebone. Speeds were quite mediocre in that nothing in excess of 71mph was reached; this maximum achieved in the Chorley Wood area. A brief signal stop outside Marylebone heralded an arrival only a few seconds down. With due respect to the Colwick staff at Nottingham it was clear No 44984 was not the engine intended to make the last run. No 44825 had indeed been cleaned up but had failed with injector trouble. Consideration had been given to running 'Jubilee' No 45562 *Alberta,* another favourite of the Midland faithful, but this was rejected on technical grounds. Whilst the crowds were inspecting No 35030 and the members of the Locomotive Club of Great Britain were saying farewell, No 44984 was making preparations for her farewell run north. This train was well known as being a newspaper train and therefore

carried 105 tons more than on the run into Marylebone. It was of course left to Driver Pavey to ease his train gently out of the platform into the tunnels for the last time. Driver Pavey bid farewell to No 44984 and the Great Central at Woodford and handed over to his colleague Driver Hutt who then took it through on the final leg to Nottingham.

Earlier in the day, the famous 16.38 had been hauled by No 45292 which again was packed with followers of the Great Central. There are many people who have memories of this train slogging away from London to Harrow-on-the-Hill. The customary chalked inscription was blazened across the smoke box door and at all the stations north small groups of people stood and watched knowing that the end was near.

One of the last cross-country services to use parts of the Great Central was the famous York–Poole through train. Again this train fell to the service of Southern Region motive power. 'West County' Pacifics Nos 34005 *Barnstaple* and 34034 *Honiton* had come into and departed respectively from Banbury, the return train being packed to 11 coaches. It had been planned to run a special for the Leicester Archeological Society to Aylesbury from Banbury and back but this had been cancelled. Gradually diesels, mainly 'Type 2s' and DMUs, began to drift into the area in readiness for the new local service that would commence from Rugby on the following Monday. How ironic that in early 1985, some 20 years after the closure of the Great Central, Marylebone station should see 'Merchant Navy' Pacific No 35028 *Clan Line,* in immaculate condition, standing at the head of a steam special sponsored by

BR taking Sunday travellers for roast beef lunches to Stratford-upon-Avon and back. Who would ever have thought in 1966 that one day 20 years on a 'Merchant Navy' would again work in and out of Marylebone.

Fortunately for preservationists, the development of the Railway Preservation Site at Quainton Road is obviously going to be a tremendous success. Home of many preserved engines, it is but a stone's throw from Aylesbury and at least is keeping steam alive for a long period of time on that area of the Great Central line which remains. Now many years on, one can still see the remnants of the Great Central. The great steel girder bridge across Rugby LWNR station still stands and one has only to venture into the countryside to see the viaducts, cuttings and some of the bridges that remain. Sadly, Woodford Halse is now all but a ghost town and indeed when the time came for the demolition of the locomotive depot at Woodford it did seem to have the last laugh in that the dynamite charges placed to blow the building up seemed to fail for the roof went up and came down again in exactly the same position in which it started. It was almost as if not only this depot but the line refused to die. It is also ironic that visit to Nottingham Victoria is now simply a visit to a major shopping centre; the only factor left which is indicative of the Great Central is the massive clock tower which has been retained. Time clearly moves on. However, on 3 September 1966, it stood still for the Great Central and has never re-started.

Above:
Class 47 diesel No D1572 passing the same location with the Poole–Newcastle train on 3 September 1966, the last day of through services over the Great Central main line. *M. Mensing*

What Followed

The End with BR

All Great Central semi-fast and long distance passenger, parcels and mail trains ceased to run after the 3 September 1966. The London Midland Region certainly wasted no time at all in getting rid of its old competitor — the contracts for demolition and track lifting were placed before the route was closed. Services did not cease altogether as a DMU service was kept to run between Nottingham Victoria and Rugby Central. After Nottingham Victoria closed in September 1967, Nottingham

Arkwright Street was hastily re-opened and the station that once saw the unloading of all Nottingham's newspapers from the Great Central 'Newspapers' train, now saw two and three car Derby and Cravens DMUs. Metro-Cammell units also made brief appearances. The DMUs ran to East Leake, Loughborough, Leicester, Ashby Magna, Lutterworth and Rugby Central. Beyond Rugby buffer stops were placed on the up and down main lines, and the track to the south was lifted with haste. Staff were withdrawn from virtually all the stations

Below:
A three-car Cravens DMU crosses the outskirts of Rugby with the 15.05 Rugby Central to Nottingham Arkwright Street on 16 April 1969. *J. Arthur*

Bottom:
A two-car DMU enters a dilapidated Leicester Central with the 17.34 service for Rugby Central on 16 April 1969.
J. Arthur

Cancels Handbill AD136

Train Service

Nottingham Arkwright Street and Rugby Central.

on and from 1 January 1968 the following service will operate.

				SO				SX
NOTTINGHAM Arkwright St. ... dep.	07 50	08 22	12 27	13 55	16 17	17 34		18 52
EAST LEAKE ... ... dep.	08 03	08 35	12 40	14 08	16 30	17 47		19 05
LOUGHBOROUGH Central ... arr.	08 10	08 42	12 47	14 15	16 37	17 54		19 12
" ... dep.	08 11	08 43	12 48	14 16	16 38	17 55		19 13
LEICESTER Central ... ... arr.	08 24	08 56	13 01	14 29	16 51	18 08		19 26
" ... dep.	08 26	08 58	13 03	14 31	16 53	18 10		19 28
ASHBY MAGNA ... ... dep.	08 41	09 13	13 18	14 46	17 08	18 25		19 43
LUTTERWORTH ... ... dep.	08 48	09 20	13 25	14 53	17 15	18 32		19 50
RUGBY Central ... ... arr.	08 57	09 29	13 34	15 02	17 24	18 41		19 59
				SO			SX	
RUGBY Central ... ... dep.	—	07 11	10 30	12 30	15 05	16 20	17 37	18 55
LUTTERWORTH ... ... dep.	—	07 20	10 39	12 39	15 14	16 29	17 46	19 04
ASHBY MAGNA ... ... dep.	—	07 28	10 47	12 47	15 22	16 37	17 54	19 12
LEICESTER Central ... ... arr.	—	07 41	11 00	13 00	15 35	16 50	18 07	19 25
" ... dep.	07 10	07 43	11 02	13 05	15 37	16 55	18 12	19 30
LOUGHBOROUGH Central arr.	07 21	07 54	11 13	13 16	15 48	17 06	18 23	19 41
" ... dep.	07 22	07 55	11 14	13 17	15 49	17 07	18 24	19 42
EAST LEAKE ... ... dep.	07 30	08 03	11 22	13 25	15 57	17 15	18 32	19 50
NOTTINGHAM Arkwright St. arr.	07 42	08 15	11 34	13 37	16 09	17 27	18 44	20 02

Notes: SO—Saturday only. SX—Saturdays excepted.

This service will provide SECOND CLASS accommodation only.

Passengers will be able to obtain tickets, **between stations served by this Service only,** from the Guard in charge of the train.

Accommodation will be provided for the conveyance of cycles, perambulators, etc., accompanied by passengers, who will be responsible for the removal of these articles from the stations.

Unaccompanied traffic will not be conveyed.

Season tickets, **between stations served by the Service only,** will be issued at Nottingham Midland, Leicester London Road and Rugby Midland Stations.

From:	Notting-ham		East Leake		Lough-boro Cen.		Leicester Central		Ashby Magna		Lutter-worth		Rugby Central	
To:	S	R	S	R	S	R	S	R	S	R	S	R	S	R
Nottingham ...			2/6	3/9	3/9	5/-	6/3	7/6	8/9	11/-	9/9	13/6	11/9	16/-
East Leake	2/6	3/9			1/4	2/6	4/3	5/6	6/6	10/-	7/9	12/-	9/6	14/6
Loughboro Central	3/9	5/-	1/4	2/6			2/9	4/6	5/6	9/-	6/3	11/3	8/3	14/3
Leicester Central ...	6/3	7/6	4/3	5/6	2/9	4/6			2/9	4/9	4/-	6/3	5/6	9/-
Ashby Magna ...	8/9	11/-	6/6	10/-	5/6	9/-	2/9	4/9			1/2	2/3	3/-	5/6
Lutterworth ...	9/9	13/6	7/9	12/-	6/3	11/3	4/-	6/3	1/2	2/3			2/-	3/9
Rugby Central ...	11/9	16/-	9/6	14/6	8/3	14/3	5/6	9/-	3/-	5/6	2/-	3/9		

The return fare quoted above is that for Cheap Day Return.

![British Rail logo] **British Rail**

London Midland Region

Issued by British Railways
Divisional Manager, Furlong House.
Middle Furlong Road, Nottingham.

AD136X   BR 35000   December, 1967

Above:
The handbill issued for the substitute service from Nottingham to Rugby introduced after the withdrawal of all through services over the Great Central main line on 3 September 1966.

Right:
Loughborough Central station after closure.
Main Line Steam Trust Ltd

and the services ran on a 'pay train' basis. Despite passing through areas of rapidly-growing population, nothing was done to re-invigorate the service in terms of marketing or public awareness. Of course that was the intention and it was only a matter of time before the Nottingham to Rugby service was withdrawn. On 5 May 1969 the last DMUs ran.

A New Beginning

Upon closure of the Great Central main line, a small group of enthusiasts known as the Main Line Preservation Group aimed to preserve the section between Nottingham and Leicester. However, due to BR needing the line for freight traffic to East Leake via a new spur connecting it to the Midland at Loughborough, the project was cut to eight miles between Loughborough Central and Belgrave and Birstall on the outskirts of Leicester.

Now known as the Main Line Steam Trust, the society attempted to buy the track and land from British Rail. Initially Loughborough Central was the sole centre for operations, but by June 1974 services were re-introduced to Quorn & Woodhouse. During this period the British Rail Property Board put increasing pressure on the Main Line Steam Trust to buy and, by April 1976, a deadline was set after which track would be removed. The public shareholding that came out of this resulted in the Great Central Railway (1976) Ltd. British Rail duly extended the deadline to June, and the Great Central Railway extended to Rothley. By May there were enough funds to buy the track at Loughborough and a single line to Quorn only. Thankfully the Borough of Charnwood helped by buying the track bed and leasing it back to the Great Central Railway for 99 years. So, following a national television and newsaper campaign, sufficient was raised to buy the single line only from Loughborough to Quorn — but Quorn to Rothley had to be paid for by January 1977, British Rail generously leaving the track in place. However, the track to the south was lifted, ostensibly to be used again elsewhere on the British Rail system. In the event it was cut up into short lengths and sold for scrap.

So what was left of the Great Central now got on with the business of running a railway. Stations, rolling stock, locomotives and signalling have gradually been restored. The Great Central Railway now has an impressive stud of locomotives, including 'B1s' Nos 1306 and 1264, 'N2' No 4744, 'Black Five' No 45231, Class 5205 2-8-0T No 5224, 'West Country' Pacific No 34039 *Boscastle*, GWR 'Hall' No 6990

Witherslack Hall and the magnificent BR Standard Class 8 Pacific No 71000 *Duke of Gloucester;* but perhaps the most famous is Great Central 4-4-0 No 506 *Butler Henderson*, the only surviving Great Central express passenger locomotive.

The Great Central (1976) Ltd has now successfully consolidated its position since the dark days of 1974. With all set fair for the future, there are two new exciting developments as regards the size of the future

Top:
A Metro-Cammell three-car DMU approaches Rugby Central with the RCTS 200th Railtour, 'The Forester', on 19 April 1969.
J.B. Hicks

Above:
A Cravens DMU passes Loughborough Central with the last Rugby Central to Nottingham Arkwright Street — the 18.55 from Rugby on 5 May 1969.
Harper Shaw

Great Central Railway. The first is the Birstall extension for which shares can now be applied. The second is the distinct possibility of running between Ruddington and East Leake stations, north of Loughborough, the eventual aim being to rebuild the bridge over the Midland at Loughborough. This will not only allow a link into British Rail, but will give one of the longest rides in the country behind a main line locomotive on a main line. It also brings the large potential markets of Nottingham and Leicester more readily in to the picture. Provided that the Great Central Railway continues to manage itself sensibly as it has always done, the original aims of the Main Line Preservation Group will be all but achieved.

Great Central Railway publicity of today invites people to join in 'The Great Adventure of the Great Central Railway'. It truly has been an adventure so far, not without its struggles, but it has certainly been very well worth while especially when *Butler Henderson's* bark is heard as she climbs away from Loughborough. Despite all the problems, the last main line has survived and will flourish again. It certainly can be claimed that, 'The Great Central Lives'.

Above:
The first steps to restoration of a section of the Great Central that will hopefully run from Ruddington to Belgrave & Birstall. The magnitude of the task is shown on 16 June 1974 as the Norwegian 2-6-0 *King Haakon* approaches with a short train from Loughborough Central to Quorn & Woodhouse.
H. A. Gamble

Right:
Restoration has progressed slowly but surely, and Great Northern Single No 1 was loaned by the National Railway Museum and is seen arriving at Rothley on the 9 May 1982. Services are now to be extended to Belgrave & Birstall and preparations are underway.   *H.A. Gamble*

Right:
Ex-Great Central 'Director' class No 506 *Butler-Henderson* stands at Rothley on 30 October 1982 prior to working back to Loughborough Central.
H.A. Gamble

Below:
Following restoration BR Standard Class 8P 4-6-2 No 71000 *Duke of Gloucester* is seen on 25 May 1986 between Loughborough and Rothley while on a steam test.
John B. Gosling